GET PUBLISHED!

How to Break into Print with a SMALL PRESS and Become RICH and FAMOUS

BRUCE FIFE

PICCADILLY BOOKS
COLORADO SPRINGS, CO

Cover design by Michael Donahue

Piccadilly Books
P.O. Box 25203
Colorado Springs, CO 80936

International sales and inquires contact:
EPS
20 Park Drive
Romford Essex RM1 4LH, UK
or
EPS
P.O. Box 1344
Studio City, CA 91614, USA

Library of Congress Cataloging-in-Publication Data
Fife, Bruce, 1952
Get published!: how to break into print with a small press and become rich and famous / Bruce Fife.
p. cm.
Includes bibliographical references and index.
ISBN 0-941599-28-0
1. Authorship--Marketing. 2. Authors and publishing. 3. Publishers and publishing. I. Title.
PN161.F43 1994
808'.02--dc20 94-17115

Simultaneously published in Australia, UK, and USA
Printed in the United States of America

CONTENTS

CHAPTER 1

YOUR DOOR TO PUBLICATION

As a writer, editor, and publisher, I have a unique perspective of the process of getting published. I have learned many of the tricks of the trade, tricks which will give you a distinct advantage in selling your work. Many of these tricks or secrets of getting published are not clearly described in other books on writing or getting published. In fact, this is the only book I know of which clearly reveals some of the most useful techniques of breaking into print.

Unlike other books on getting published, this one is written specifically for new writers. Other books on the subject present a somewhat biased view designed more for seasoned authors seeking publication with the publishing giants, who, by the way, rarely consider material from unpublished writers. Although these books are helpful, they do not offer practical advice for newcomers or paint a realistic picture of the process of breaking into print. A beginning writer must approach the process of getting published from a different angle. Recognizing this fact, I have written this book with the beginning writer in mind.

This book contains the standard information all writers need to know in order to get published. It also includes valuable information which will give you the edge over other writers and direct you to the publishers most likely to publish your work. You will learn how to avoid the mistakes most beginning writers make in preparing and submitting manuscripts. You will discover the secrets of finding and approaching the publishers who would be most interested in your material.

It is a sad fact of life that most publishers are prejudiced against new writers. If you are not already a published author, editors will pay little attention to your material. Many will refuse to even look at it! They actually try to avoid new writers. Busy editors would rather spend their time reading material submitted by established authors.

It seems that unless you are already a published author (or a celebrity), your chances of breaking into print are slim. However, this is not really true. It appears that way only because most new writers don't know which publishers to approach or how to approach them properly. You don't need to be an award-winning writer or a literary genius to sell your writing. The truth is: If you have *average* writing skills, you *can* get published! This book will show you how to overcome editors' built-in resistance to new writers and how to find the publishers who will be most receptive to you.

This book contains a realistic and practical approach to breaking into print. Other books focus on getting published by the big publishing companies, which is really unrealistic for new writers. The vast majority of new writers break into print with small presses. If you spend all your time trying to get your big break with a large press, you will be greatly disappointed, become discouraged, and likely remain unpublished.

It is a well-known fact that large publishers are prejudiced against new authors. The chances for unpublished writers getting published by them are astronomical. They, as well as literary agents, prefer to work with people who have already had several books published.

The only way most unpublished authors are going to get published is with the small or independent presses, who are much more receptive to new writers. It is with the small publishers that new writers can get the opportunity to work with editors, hone their skills, and eventually break into the world of print. Small publishers provide a valuable service for new authors by helping them develop their writing skills and publishing their works. They are the ones who cultivate new talent and open the door to publishing opportunities.

This book describes many fascinating facts about the benefits of being published by a small press. Not only will authors find more success in getting published, but they have the potential to make a great deal more money than they would with the large publishers. Yes, being published by a small press can be much more rewarding for you financially.

I have seen no book on the market adequately address these issues. Some texts will mention small presses briefly as an alternative means to getting published. These books are fine for writers who have already had some degree of success, but for most unpublished authors they are of little real value. In this book, breaking into print with the small press is a major focus. If you are a new writer and want to learn the easiest and quickest way to become published with the greatest financial possibilities, then this will be the most valuable book you could read.

Chapters 2 and 4, explain the two major keys or secrets to getting published. Chapter 3 explains how to find the markets for your book. Chapters 4 and 5 describe the markets in more detail, and how to approach them. Chapter 4 focuses on book publishing, and Chapter 5 on magazine articles. Chapters 6, 7, 8, and 9 discuss the submission process in detail—how to properly write, prepare, and submit query letters, book proposals, and manuscripts, with examples of each. Chapter 10 discusses the pros and cons of using an agent. I've included Chapter 11, on additional markets, so that you will know what other options are available. Chapter 12 discusses some of the things you can do to improve the quality of your writing, become more professional, and enhance your chances of getting published. The Appendix lists many books, magazines, organizations, and market resources that will help you improve your writing skills and increase the chances of selling your work.

A Success Story

If it wasn't for her enthusiasm for the subject, first-time author Julie Strasser would have never finished writing *Swoosh: The Unauthorized Story of Nike and the Men Who Played There*. Strasser, who was formerly Nike's advertising manager, began the book in the mid 1980s. The book describes the company's shaky start in the early 1960s, when it sold sneakers out of car trunks, to its rise to the number one spot in the athletic shoe industry.

Writing the book took more than half a decade. Several times Strasser felt like giving up. Nike employees, fearing retribution, avoided talking with her. Phil Knight, the company founder, refused to be interviewed and told her he wanted a "real writer" to do the book. Discouraged, she had second thoughts about completing the manuscript and put it aside.

Nike had overcome many obstacles to achieve success. In its early years banks threw company officials out, factories turned down their orders, and stock analysts laughed at them. Determined to succeed they overcame these obstacles to challenge their competitors who dominated the industry. Strasser reasoned that if a small struggling company can overcome the odds and succeed, so could she.

Her sister Laurie Becklund, a *Los Angeles Times* reporter, joined her and wrote the track and field section, but Strasser did the rest.

Strasser sent a book proposal and several completed chapters to a top literary agent in New York. The agent said the book didn't have a chance stating, "Who cares about these guys from Oregon and their shoes?"

She felt like putting the manuscript away permanently, but she knew she had a good story. Ignoring the agent's advice she spent another two years researching, polishing, and perfecting the book. She pored over hundreds of pages of notes compiled from countless sources that encompassed court records, personal accounts, published articles, and government documents.

Her hard work and determination paid off. She sold the book receiving an advance of $200,000, an enormous amount for a first-time author. Released in 1991, *Swoosh* became a bestseller.

Strasser is just one of dozens of first-time authors who have made it big in recent years. If you asked these authors what contributed to their success, it would boil down to five basic elements:

1. Interest. Write on a subject you know about or would like to learn about, and you will write with enthusiasm that will interest readers.

2. Devotion. Spend the time necessary to adequately research your subject. A thoroughly researched book may take years to write.

3. Polish and Refine. Reread and rewrite your material as often as necessary to make it the best it can possibly be.

4. Professionalism. Follow the proper procedures of preparing and submitting manuscripts.

5. Perseverance. Don't take rejection personally and don't give up.

CHAPTER 2

MISTAKES BEGINNERS MAKE

The chances of a novice writer getting published are very slim. Fewer than one out of every 100 submissions sent to book publishers ever sell. This includes material from novice writers as well as people like Stephen King and James Michener. An unpublished writer's chances are probably less than one in 1000. Why is it so hard for a new author to get published?

Publishers, as a whole, are prejudiced against new writers, and for good reason. Most unpublished authors do not understand what it takes to become published. Publishing is a business, the business of producing and selling books and magazines. Most publishers want to produce quality products that will earn a profit. Turning out products that are filled with errors or have little customer appeal would drive the company out of business. Publishers of necessity must be very selective.

WHY MANUSCRIPTS ARE REJECTED

You spend months slaving away, writing what you consider to be an intriguing novel or useful nonfiction book. You rewrite and polish the wording and phraseology until it is eloquent and interesting. You have faith in your work. You know it can sell well, and perhaps be a candidate for the bestseller list. But it is rejected by publisher after publisher. What's the matter? Can't publishers recognize a potential bestseller when they see it?

Whether the book can become a bestseller is anybody's guess. Publishers have experience to tell them which books can and cannot sell, and which ones will sell the best. However, they cannot accurately predict the sales potential of every manuscript they receive. Consequently, some bestselling books have been rejected by a multitude of publishers before being sold.

If a book obviously has bestseller potential, why doesn't every publisher jump at the chance to buy it? Can the professional judgment of so many editors be wrong? Not usually. Occasionally editors will pass by a masterfully written work simply because the subject material is new or different and the editors do not have experience with similar books to accurately compare it to. Therefore, it may be rejected. However, most manuscripts are rejected for a number of very good reasons.

The following situations describe why manuscripts are rejected.

Improper Submission Format

One major reason for rejection is that the material is not properly prepared, or is not submitted in the correct format. If the manuscript looks sloppy, is not double-spaced, or lacks slug lines, it will not be taken seriously. Publishers feel that if the author is not serious enough to take the time to prepare and submit the manuscript properly, it will probably not be well researched or will be written in a careless manner. Many editors refuse to consider any material that is not submitted in the proper format. Or if a publisher requires that a query letter or book proposal be sent to them before receiving the manuscript, any manuscript sent first will automatically be rejected.

Some editors will consider submissions with slight deviations from standard format and submission procedures, if the material shows promise. An author, however, should never allow his or her material to be rejected simply because it was not properly prepared or submitted. There are many resource materials available which explain how to prepare and submit manuscripts, including Chapters 6, 7, 8, and 9 in this book.

Lack of Writing Skills

Poor writing is another major reason manuscripts are rejected. Most novice writers simply do not write well enough to get published. I'm not talking just about grammar and mechanics, but about conveying information in a manner that is instructive, easy-to-understand, and enjoyable to read.

As a publisher, I receive some manuscripts on topics my publishing company is very much interested in, written by people who have a great deal of knowledge on the subject. Unfortunately, I often am forced to reject these manuscripts because the authors cannot adequately express themselves or their knowledge in words. The quality of their writing is so poor that the material is of little value.

Good writing requires both talent and skill, with the greatest emphasis on skill. If you have a little talent in a particular field, you can usually master the skills necessary to work in and be successful in that field. It is the same for writing. You can develop the skills to become a good writer. All professional writers began as unpublished authors. Their works weren't automatically acclaimed as great literary masterpieces. They struggled, practiced, studied, and learned how to craft their ideas, organize their thoughts, and do the research necessary to become successful writers. Successful writers are not born, they are made.

A writer with average writing skills, however, can get published if he or she goes about it wisely. I will show you how in succeeding chapters. I will also show you how to improve your writing, and to make it the best it can possibly be.

Wrong Publisher

Submitting material to the wrong publisher is another common reason for manuscripts being rejected. Contrary to popular belief, publishers will not publish a book simply because it looks like a bestseller. Every publishing house has its own areas of specialization, with its own viewpoint or focus. Each will publish only those books that fit its personality and areas of specialization. Large publishing companies have a wide range of interests, and publish many different types of books. These large companies will often have subsidiary publishing companies, known as imprints, which specialize in certain types of books. For instance, Del Rey Books, an imprint of Ballantine Books, specializes in fantasy and science fiction novels.

Smaller publishing companies have fewer subject interests. Broadway Press, for example, is only interested in books on theater and performing arts. Backcountry Publications is interested only in outdoor recreation topics. If you send a potential bestselling romance novel to Better Homes and Gardens Books, or an entertaining children's picture book to Career Press, you will be rejected. I have chosen obvious examples here to illustrate my point, but in most cases you cannot tell what types of books a company specializes in just by its name.

Many novice writers, not knowing any better, will simply look for addresses of publishers by thumbing through books lying around the house. Writers with a little more forethought will try to find books that are similar to the ones they have written, believing that the publisher will also be interested in their book as well. This is better than randomly sending out manuscripts, but there is a better way. Directories are available which list publishers and describe exactly what types of books they are looking for. (I will discuss this more in Chapter 3.) With this type of information readily available, no writer should send a publisher something he is not interested in.

There are some writers who disregard this advice and will still send material to any publisher. They feel their work is so good that any publisher will want it, and they knowingly submit it to inappropriate publishers. They will state in their cover letter something like, "I know you don't normally publish this type of book, but after you read it you will see it has the potential to become a bestseller..." It doesn't matter how good the manuscript is, if it is not what the company publishes, they won't be interested.

Limited Customer Interest

You may produce a well-written book on a topic that interests you. However, if there are not enough people willing to buy a book on that topic, the manuscript won't find a publisher. If the publisher cannot sell enough books to make a profit, he is not going to publish the book, no matter how good it is.

A book titled *The Yummy Liver Cookbook*, for instance, would have little appeal to most people and would not sell well in normal distribution channels. The same is true for a book about New Zealand politics. There is no demand for such books in this country.

I am sent many autobiographies from novice writers. The authors of these works are not famous, but average people, working typical jobs who feel a need to tell their stories and express their thoughts on life. Unfortunately for them, this type of book will not sell. The average reader is not particularly interested in the day-to-day life of an auto mechanic or a stenographer. Unless you are a celebrity of some sort, most people will not be interested in reading your life story. Granted, there may be some exceptions for people who have led colorful lives, but their stories must be written with the skill of a professional writer to make them interesting and publishable.

Some books with limited customer interest could be profitable if produced and marketed by the right publisher. Even though a huge company like Prentice-Hall publishes some performing arts books, one on television camera operation is too narrow a subject for them. However, Players Press, which specializes in theater books, might be very interested. Players Press has a market for this type of book because their distribution channels service theatrical markets. But even Players Press would be more interested in books that have a wider appeal and potentially larger sales.

Overworked Subject

The first few good books published on a new popular subject will always be the most successful. As more books on the subject are published, the competition for customers increases, adversely effecting the sales of all the books. After all, if a customer is interested in learning how to decorate cakes, and buys a book on the subject, she is not likely to buy a second one. If there are too many books already in print on a particular subject, a publisher will not be excited about publishing another. The competition is simply too great to take the risk.

It seems that once a book hits the bestseller list, everyone jumps on the bandwagon and writes copycat books. This often results in the writing and publication of some mediocre books. Most copycat books do not match the original book's writing quality and content.

Most clones of popular books are not as successful as the original. In fact, I have seen books that are superior to bestsellers but do not do as well because they came out after the original. They do not get the reviews or have the prestige of being the original book on the subject. When faced with a choice between two books on the same subject, people will most likely choose the book that has had more publicity, which most likely will be the first book.

When a new type of book hits the bestseller list I am flooded with copycats. A couple of examples readily come to mind. One is *Millie's Book: As Dictated to Barbara Bush,* which was written from the viewpoint of the First Family's pet dog, Millie. When it became a bestseller, I was deluged with other books credited to dogs, cats, fish, and other pets. After the publication of Barbara Kipfer's bestselling *14,000 Things to Be Happy About*, I received a sudden influx of books taking the opposite approach, such as *5,000 Things to Be Crabby About.* After a few months these books are gone, and so is the interest in that subject.

If the author and publisher are lucky, a book will be published just as a new trend or craze is beginning to become popular. These trends are very unpredictable. They may last only a few months, or as long as several years. The books that become successful are the ones published as the trends are still growing in popularity. Once a trend has hit its peak and public interest starts to decline, publishers are not interested in producing new books on the subject. It takes nearly a year after a book has been accepted for publication before it is actually available for sale. A fad that was popular when the book is submitted for publication may be dead by the time it is published. This is another reason why publishers are very cautious about publishing new books on popular new trends when other books are already available.

Most of what I have said here deals with nonfiction books and articles, but the same is true for novels and short stories. Some subjects and plots are retold over and over again. Publishers want something new and exciting, not a rehash of something already done. Be original.

Economics of Publishing

With the exception of university presses, most book publishers are in business to make money. They make most of their money by selling books. The more books they sell, the more profit they make. Publishers are not particularly interested in works with great literary, academic, or social value. They want products that will sell and sell well. Therefore, their primary aim is to find and publish material with the greatest potential market.

Most writers have little concept of what can be profitably published. Marketing is of secondary interest to them. They usually write on subjects that they are personally interested in, with little regard to its marketing potential. Publishers aren't going to throw their money around carelessly. They look for the books that they believe have the greatest chance of success.

Although publishers reject the vast majority of material they receive, not all of this material is unpublishable. They receive many good manuscripts that could possibly be profitable. But because most publishing companies operate on a narrow profit margin, they simply cannot publish every good book they receive. Therefore, book publishers must select those books which they feel have the greatest chance of making the most money. Magazine publishers must choose articles they believe will be of greatest interest to their readers, and will help sell their publications.

Publishing is a blend of business sense and intuition that varies from one editor to the next. In deciding which books to accept for publication, book publishers rely on estimates of the books' sales potential and their editors' enthusiasm for the manuscript. If an editor likes the manuscript, she may convince her company to publish it. One editor may highly recommend a particular manuscript, while another editor may hate it. Personal preference often decides if a book gets published or not. However, a well-written and interesting manuscript is more likely to find an enthusiastic editor to endorse it than one that is not.

Editors are not always right. On rare occasions they reject manuscripts that later become bestsellers. But as professionals familiar with book publishing, they do have an inside track on what types of books sell. And for the most part they do a good job at picking out the best books for their companies. Simply because a book was rejected does not mean the editor did not like it or that it did not have sales potential. If the book did not conform to the publication's viewpoint or fit in with its list of books, it would be rejected regardless of how good it was.

THE NOVICE WRITER

It is a fact of life that publishers are prejudiced against unpublished writers. Material from new writers is looked upon very critically and often rejected simply because it was produced by an amateur. This may sound unjustly biased, but in all fairness, publishers have justifiable reasons for being skeptical of unpublished writers.

It is the unpublished writer who commonly makes the mistakes discussed earlier in this chapter. Published authors, in general, do not make these mistakes; that is why they are published. Their writing skills are usually much better. They can express themselves and their thoughts effectively. Experienced writers also know how to properly prepare and submit query letters and manuscripts. They are aware of what is happening in the world, and have a feel for what type of material is marketable and to whom it will sell. They present themselves in a businesslike and professional manner. In essence, getting published all boils down to professionalism. A published author is considered a "professional," and his or her material is given more serious consideration.

One of the primary keys to getting your work published is to get over the barrier of being classified as a "novice writer." If you are a published author, your submissions will receive the attention a professional writer deserves. You avoid the first round of rejections which eliminate perhaps 90 percent of the material publishers receive.

You might be thinking: If I'm not a published writer yet, how can I become one if publishers reject material from unpublished authors? My answer is that you don't need to be a published author in order to *look* like one. Keep in mind that as a writer you are producing a product, your manuscript, which you are trying to sell to a publishing company. To be successful, you must approach the processes of selling your writing in a professional, businesslike manner. If you present yourself and your material like a professional would, you will be treated like a professional writer. Conversely, if you present yourself like an amateur, you will be treated like one.

In this chapter you have learned the mistakes that beginners make and the reasons why manuscripts are rejected: improper submission format, poor writing, submitting to the wrong publisher, selecting an overworked subject, limited customer interest, and economics. Except for economics, you have almost total control over these conditions. Therefore, you can eliminate these reasons for rejection by preparing and submitting your material as a professional would. Even with economics, you do have some control. If you produce a well-written manuscript that is of interest to many people, you will find enthusiastic editors who will want to publish it.

In summary, one of the essential keys to getting published is to make yourself look like a professional writer. I will explain in detail how you do this in coming chapters.

Although I emphasize selling book-length manuscripts in this chapter, much of what I said applies to writing magazine articles as well. Magazine articles will be covered more specifically in Chapter 5.

CHAPTER 3

THE MARKETS

As you learned in the previous chapter, one of the things you don't want to do is to send your manuscript to just any publisher. That is a waste of your time and money. There are many thousands of book and magazine publishers in North America. Without direction you could spend your lifetime trying to find the right one. In this chapter I will show you how to locate the proper markets for your books and articles.

I receive calls all the time from local unpublished authors who have written books but don't know what to do next. They have no idea how to approach a publisher or even who to approach. The quickest and most helpful advice I can give them is to go down to their local library or bookstore and look at a copy of one of the publisher directories. These books will give them everything they need to know to get started.

There are several different directories available which list book and magazine publishers, as well as many other services and businesses associated with the publishing industry. In these directories you will find the names and addresses of publishers, as well as learn about the types of material they publish. This will help you locate the right publisher for your work. If you want to get published, you should become very familiar with these resources and use the valuable information they contain.

WRITER'S MARKET

The most valuable publisher directory for writers is *Writer's Market.* It is your guide to all the book and periodical publishers in the United States and Canada who purchase material from freelance writers. In it you can find information on over 4,000 publishers (800 book publishers, 3,200 magazine publishers), their names, addresses, and descriptions of the types of material they publish. It tells you where to sell articles, books, fillers, greeting cards, novels, plays, scripts, and short stories. All knowledgeable writers and literary agents use it as their primary marketing reference. Because there are so many changes in the publishing industry—new companies start up, others go out of business, names and addresses change—this book is updated and a new edition is published every year.

Before searching for a publisher you should refer to *Writer's Market.* Don't send your manuscript until you have referred to this directory first. One of the primary reasons manuscripts are rejected is that the subject material is not appropriate for that publisher.

If you have written a travel guide to the state of Vermont you won't get it published by *Children's Press* or *Financial Sourcebooks,* so you shouldn't even try them. This example may sound obvious to you, but believe me it is not far-fetched. The publishing company I work for has a very narrow rage of interest, yet I receive manuscripts on every subject from cooking eggplant to belly dancing. If these authors had refered to *Writer's Market* first, they wouldn't have wasted their time and money sending us this stuff. No matter how good a book may be, we're not interested unless it fits our publishing program.

Many unpublished authors send their work to any publisher. They reason that since their book is a potential bestseller, any publisher will jump at the chance to publish it. Not true. While most unpublished authors believe they have just written the next #1 bestseller, the vast majority of these works will never be printed. Why? Partly because the author doesn't know where to find the right publisher or how to approach him.

Turning back to our example, if you have a travel guide on Vermont you will need to find a publisher interested not only in travel topics, but specifically traveling in Vermont. Just because you have found a publisher who has published a travel book on Southern California does not mean he will be interested in a similar book on Vermont. His interest may be limited to California or the Southwest. You need to find out what the publisher wants. You do this by referring to *Writer's Market.*

Besides describing the types of books and articles they publish, *Writer's Market* also provides the publisher's most current addresses, the specific editors' names, the number of books published each year or the magazines' circulation size, the type of submissions they want, the time they require to evaluate submissions, and more. All of this information is important to you if you want to sell your writing.

To give you a better understanding of the information contained in *Writer's Market*, on the following page I have provided an example of a typical listing, along with a brief explanation of the content. (I have added the numbers for explanatory purposes.)

At the back of the book section is a subject index. If your manuscript is about dogs, you would turn to the index and look under the heading of "Animals" for publishers who publish books on animals. You then look them up in the book publishers section, which is in alphabetical order. No matter what the subject of your manuscript, using the subject index you can locate publishers likely to be interested. This will save you from thumbing through each of the 800 listings.

The listing of magazine publishers is basically the same as that of the book publishers. Information which may also be included with a magazine is frequency of publication, circulation size, which rights are purchased, average article length, whether photos are accepted and the type desired, percentage of articles

(1) **BRUNSWICK PRESS,** P.O. Box 43545, Los Angeles CA 95601. (818) 472-2332. Fax (818) 472-5645. **(2)** Editor: Frank Bellows. **(3)** Estab. 1963. **(4)** Publishes hardcover and trade paperback originals and reprints. **(5)** Averages 25-35 titles/year; receives 500 submissions annually; 80% of books from first-time authors; 90% of books from unagented writers. **(6)** Average print order for a writer's first book is 5,000. **(7)** Pays 5-10% royalty on retail price. Offers average $1,000 advance. **(8)** Publishes book an average of 10 months after acceptance. **(9)** Simultaneous submissions OK. **(10)** Query for electronic submissions. **(11)** Reports in 1 month on queries; 2 months on mss. **(12)** Submit outline/synopsis and first 3 chapters or complete ms. **(13)** Book catalog and manuscript guidelines for #10 SASE.
(14) **Nonfiction**: Children's and young adult books, biography, humor, juvenile, picture books. Animals, sports, history, nature, science, games.
(15) **Recent Nonfiction Title:** *Science Fun*, by Robert Smith
(16) **Fiction:** Adventure, fantasy, historical, humor, juvenile, mystery, picture books, suspense. Looking for humorous fiction for ages 7-11.
(17) **Recent Fiction Title:** *Space Cadet*, by Susan Elkins.
(18) **Tips:** Our audience consists mostly of youth ages 7-16; we are not interested in material for older readers.

Explanation:
(1) The name of the company, current address, and phone number.
(2) The current editor to whom you should address your submission.
(3) Year the company was established. An older company generally implies a more stable business.
(4) An explanation of the types of material published.
(5) The number of new books published each year. The number of submissions received and from whom. Can indicate whether or not the company is receptive to new or unagented writers.
(6) The number of books in the average first printing.
(7) Royalty and advance information.
(8) Length of time after acceptance before the book is in print.
(9) Will accept simultaneous submissions.
(10) Indicates whether they will accept submissions sent over a modem or on a computer diskette.
(11) Reporting time on query letters and manuscripts.
(12) Submission requirements. Indicates whether they want a query letter, a detailed book proposal, the complete manuscript, or some combination of these.
(13) A copy of the publisher's author guidelines or a copy of his catalog is available. Some companies offer it free; others request a self-addressed stamped #10 business-size envelope.
(14) Nonfiction topics of interest.
(15) Recent nonfiction title published.
(16) Fiction topics of interest.
(17) Recent fiction title published.
(18) Includes any additional information the publisher wants prospective writers to know.

Example and explanation of a *Writer's Market* listing

which are by freelancers, and specific characteristics about the material each publishes.

There is no periodical publisher subject index at the back of the book because the publications are all listed under specific subject headings throughout the directory. So if you want to write an article on skiing, look in the table of contents at the front of the directory in the Consumer Publications section under the heading "Sports." Under that is the subheading "Skiing and Snow Sports." You will find the magazines that would be most interested in your article on the pages indicated.

After you have chosen a few publishers who publish the type of material you have written, write to them and request their writer's guidelines. These guidelines will contain the most current and detailed information concerning the type of material they publish, and explain how they want to receive submissions. Some guidelines are very specific, while others are more generalized. Many will specify how to prepare your manuscript. One publisher may want it set up one way, while another may request it in a completely different format. In Chapter 8, I will show you the commonly accepted formats for manuscripts. However, you may find publishers who will request something slightly different. If they don't specify, use the examples as described in this book.

LITERARY MARKET PLACE

Another important directory you should become familiar with is *Literary Market Place.* It contains a comprehensive listing of nearly 2,000 pages of publishers, book producers (packagers), editorial services, literary agents, marketing and publicity firms, book manufacturers, distributors, trade associations, photographers, translators, consultants, illustrators, trade publications, workshops, and almost any other kind of service or company involved in the book publishing trade. Many of these services can be invaluable in getting your work prepared for publication (see Chapter 12 for additional information on literary services).

Literary Market Place is updated and published annually. It lists about 3,700 publishers, and includes a small press section. Book publishers are required to publish an average of at least three new books per year in order to be included in the main Book Publishers section. Publishers who do not fit this criteria may be listed in the Small Press section for a fee.

Unlike *Writer's Market,* the publishers listed in *Literary Market Place* include both those who actively look for and buy material from freelance writers and those who do not. Some companies are not included in *Writer's Market* because they specifically asked not to be listed. The reasons are that they receive too many unsolicited submissions or they do not accept any unagented submissions.

The entries in *Literary Market Place* generally include name, address, phone number, key personnel, brief description of types of books published, number of titles printed in previous year, total number currently in print, and year founded. It contains a more detailed listing of key personnel than *Writer's Market,* but the description of the types of books published and what each publisher is looking for is not as comprehensive.

The main publisher listings are in alphabetical order. Following this are geographic (state by state), type (scholarly, trade, mass market paperback, hardcover, etc.), and subject indexes. The Canadian book publishers section follows.

Literary Market Place is a large and expensive book (priced at about $160). For this reason it is best that you go to your library to use it. It is usually shelved in the reference section of the library and probably cannot be checked out, so you must use it in the library.

Another book you may be interested in, which is very similar to *Literary Market Place* and published by the same company, is *International Literary Market Place.* It contains the same type of information as *Literary Market Place* for companies and services outside the United States and Canada. Foreign publishers may be another market you can pursue if your book is specifically suitable for them or if domestic publishers show little interest.

OTHER DIRECTORIES

There are many other publisher directories available, some of which may be more appropriate to your needs than either *Writer's Market* or *Literary Market Place.*

Writer's Market contains a lot of information of interest to writers of various materials including books of all types, magazines and trade journal articles, greeting cards, plays, etc. *Literary Market Place* is of primary interest to authors of books. The publishers of *Writer's Market* also produce a series of references aimed at more specific markets. If you're interested in selling poetry, for example, you can look in *Poet's Market.* Other books available include *Children's Writer's & Illustrator's Market, Children's Media Market Place, Religious Writer's Marketplace, Novel and Short Story Writer's Market, Scriptwriters Market,* and *Humor and Cartoon Markets,* among others. These books are all laid out in a format similar to *Writer's Market* and include both book and periodical publishers.

An excellent comprehensive directory of small publishing companies is the *International Directory of Little Magazines and Small Presses.* This reference contains both very small publishers and self-publishers, as well as moderate-sized companies. Listings of book publishers include the year founded, the number of books published each year, and the number of books each publisher currently has in print, which gives a good idea of the company's size and stability. Magazine listings include frequency of publication, circulation size, and topics of interest. Subject and geographic indexes are also included.

Both American and Canadian publishers are listed in most of the directories mentioned above. Some directories are devoted entirely to Canadian publishers. They are *Canadian Publishers Directory, The Book Trade in Canada/L'Industrie du Livre au Canada, The Canadian Writer's Guide,* and *The Canadian Writer's Market.* Another source which lists publishers in North America, the British Commonwealth, and other countries is *International Writer's and Artist's Yearbook.* See the Appendix for additional resources.

There are several periodical directories, such as *The Standard Periodical Directory, The Serials Directory,* and *Ulriche's International Periodicals Directory,* to name a few. These directories list many thousands of magazines, trade journals, and newsletters, but do not provide much useful information about the types of material they publish. They are good for locating addresses and getting a general idea of their subject areas, but that is about it. The market directories listed earlier are much better resources and the ones you should rely on.

CHAPTER 4

CHOOSING A BOOK PUBLISHER

In this chapter I will explain how to approach your markets—the publishers. You will learn which markets are most receptive to new writers and how to earn the greatest profits. You will learn essential information about the process of preparing and submitting your work to publishers.

WHY BOOK PUBLISHERS ARE SO SELECTIVE

Although the vast majority of the material publishers receive is unpublishable, they also receive a lot of well-written, publishable material. However, because of economic restraints, they cannot publish every good book they receive. I will explain some of the reasons for this in the following sections.

Too Little Time

Editors as a whole are underpaid and overworked. Most of them must take work home daily just to keep from falling behind.

In search for better working environments and the chance to get even a small raise, editors frequently jump from company to company. This is unfortunate for the authors working with these editors, as new editors, lacking the same enthusiasm for the author's work, may eventually cancel books that were accepted by their predecessors.

Editors spend most of their time preparing books contracted for publication. This includes attending scheduling and sales meetings; writing jacket and catalog copy; composing sales information sheets; editing current projects; coordinating cover design, illustrations, and text; dealing with authors (who can be demanding and troublesome, especially those of celebrity status); and all the various minor activities that these functions entail. These duties eat up most of an eight-hour work day, leaving little time for reading and evaluating new manuscripts. For this reason, editors must focus their time on the most promising material that comes across their desks—material from successful authors they have worked with in the past, and authors who present themselves as published professionals with marketable products. Editors cannot afford the luxury of browsing through every submission at a leisurely pace in search for the few publishable works among the hundreds that continually stream in. As a result, many good books from first time authors are rejected without a proper evaluation.

Too Little Profit

If editors are so busy that they let good books slip by, why don't publishers hire more editors? Wouldn't catching all these good books add to the company's overall profits? Unfortunately, no.

Publishing is not as lucrative as you might believe. It's tough to make money in publishing. Many companies go out of business each year. In fact, some industries in this country spend more on just their advertising than the entire book industry earns in profit. You hear about large advances paid to some authors for their books and reason that if publishers can afford to pay that kind of money, they must be loaded. Not true. You only hear about these large advances because they are so rare, and only a few of the large publishing giants can afford to give them.

Publishers give discounts to wholesalers, distributors, and book dealers which amount to an average of about 45 percent off the retail price. Prepress and manufacturing costs may account for 20 percent or more. Author royalties take out another 10 percent or so. Operating expenses (which include editor's salaries, marketing, administrative costs, and other overhead expenses) amount to about 20 percent. These are essential expenses that must be met, leaving about five percent for promotion, advertising, and profit. For the initial printing of a book, the publisher's profit amounts to only a small fraction of the retail price.*

To make matters worse, most books are sold on a returnable basis. This means that if the books do not sell, the book dealer can return them for full credit. About 25 percent of all hardcover books and up to 50 percent of paperbacks are eventually returned. Many of these books, damaged by shipping or shop wear, are unsalable or salable only at steep discounts. For mass market paperbacks, the store owners tear off and return only the covers, disposing of the rest of the book.

I know of no other industry where dealers can return unsold products to the manufacturer and, in some cases, even destroy them and get full credit. But this is what happens in the publishing industry.

Too Much Competition

There are approximately one million books currently in print and available for sale in this country. Every year over 147,000 new English-language books are published and distributed in the United States and Canada. Although this may sound encour-

---

*These percentages represent an estimated average for medium- and large-sized publishing companies. Exact figures will vary depending on a number of factors, including the efficiency with which the company is run. These figures are also based on the first printing of a book. Reprints of successful books are cheaper to produce because prepress expenses are eliminated and press runs increased, making production more economical, so the profit margin would be slightly better.

aging to authors (more chances of getting published), it is really detrimental. With a million other books on the market, each new book must compete against them for limited shelf space in stores, editorial space in the media, publisher's promotional dollars, and ultimately customers.

Competition can, and does, destroy the sales of many books. If, for instance, there was only one Chinese cookbook in print, it would probably sell very well. All things being equal, if this book had to compete with 30 other books on the same subject, its sales would decrease by a factor of 30. From a publishing standpoint, this could make *all* of these cookbooks unprofitable.

An average size bookstore may stock 30,000-50,000 books. If you were a bookstore owner, which books would you choose? You have a million to choose from, and 147,000 new ones coming out each year. Like most store owners you would choose those that have made the bestseller lists and those that have continually sold well over the years. Most of the books will be older books that have proven to be good sellers. Only a fraction of the space in bookstores is given to new titles. The vast majority of new books don't even see the inside of most bookstores. The obvious result is poor sales for many books which, consequently, go out of print. Most new books go out of print after the first printing.

Publishers know that new books are a risk, so they normally limit the number of books in the first printing to about 5,000-10,000 copies (this is trade hardcover books—books typically sold in bookstores, not little mass market paperbacks, directories, encyclopedias, professional works, or textbooks). Some companies' initial average print runs will be a little more, others a little less. You may hear of print runs significantly larger, but these are the exception and not the general rule. Larger print runs are reserved for those titles that the publisher feels confident will become bestsellers—those written by big name authors and film stars. The big publishing companies need to sell approximately 5,000-10,000 copies in order to break even on the expenses of producing and marketing a new book. So, for most books the typical print run is limited to about 5,000-10,000 copies. If they can sell more than this amount within the first year, the book will probably make them a profit. If the book does not sell this initial printing after about a year, it is usually considered a financial loss and is taken out of print. While a book that sells just over 5,000 copies or so may be a marginal success, a bestseller is one that sells upwards of 30,000 or more. To make the big time bestseller lists, a book would need to sell three or four times that amount.

Too Many Failures

Here are some facts that may surprise you. Eighty percent of all new books will not be profitable enough to reprint. That's an 80 percent failure rate! This means that publishers make their profit on only 20 percent of the new books published. (Of course, this is in addition to reprints of books that have proven successful in previous years.) Of the 20 percent which are profitable, only a few could be considered bestsellers, and far fewer than that ever make the big time bestseller lists. It's no wonder publishing companies struggle financially.

The big publishing companies make their profits on relatively few titles. This means they must be very selective in the books they choose to publish. It means they cannot publish every good manuscript they receive. The publisher must choose those books that have the greatest profit potential. If the publisher had to decide between two books, one of which is a literary masterpiece and one of which is not, but has greater marketing potential, which one will he publish? The second one, the one that will make him the most money.

In Search of the Bestseller

For the reasons discussed above, publishers, particularly the big publishing companies, focus on publishing bestsellers (those that they believe will sell over 20,000 or 30,000 copies). Their survival depends on finding the next bestseller. This is a very important concept for writers to understand because it affects what publishers will buy. They are not particularly interested in a good book with the potential to sell just a few thousand copies. They want blockbusters, books with mass appeal. They want books written by celebrities, or about celebrities or other famous people. They want books that cater to new popular trends, or that correspond to current economic and political events, before public interest has reached its peak. They have a tendency to ignore new authors and concentrate on works from established writers who have already made names for themselves, books by literary superstars which will automatically be successful because these authors have built up reputations and faithful followings. Publishers take a greater risk when dealing with an unknown author. For this reason, many of the large publishing houses will not even consider an author who has not already had several books published. They will accept works by famous nonwriters, such as popular athletes, politicians, entertainers, and the like. But they will assign a competent co-author to do the majority of the writing. If you or your book doesn't fit into these categories, it will be extremely difficult for you to get published by the large publishing houses.

All book publishing companies are flooded with unsolicited submissions, particularly the large publishers who are more visible to the general public. As a result, most of the large publishing companies, and many medium-sized companies, will not even look at a submission unless it is handled by a literary agent. Manuscripts received directly from authors are automatically returned unread. So, to even approach one of these companies you need to have an agent. Experienced writers will tell you, however, that it is just as difficult to find an agent willing to work with you as it is to find a publisher. Agents do not like to work with unpublished writers any more than publishers do. Most agents look for writers who have already had two or three books published. New writers, it appears, can't get published unless they work with an agent, but agents won't work with them unless they have already been published. It seems like a no-win situation. As dismal as all this may appear, it really isn't that bad, that is, not if you know the next key to getting published, which I will explain to you in the following section.

THE BEST KEPT SECRET IN PUBLISHING

If you want to get published, this section will be one of the most important you will read. I have not seen the information contained in this section and the rest of this chapter adequately explained in any other source. I will show you how you can save a lot of time and effort, avoid heartache, and earn the most profit possible with your writing.

It seems that everybody wants to have their book published by one of the big well-known publishing houses. These large companies are collectively referred to as the "New York" publishers because most of the country's biggest publishing houses are headquartered in New York City. The general feeling among unpublished authors is that they need to have one of the large New York publishers buy their books in order to receive the recognition they desire and royalties that will make them rich.

For some reason, writers believe that the larger the publishing company, the more money they will get for their work. Or perhaps, since these giants publish hundreds of new titles every year, their chances of getting accepted are increased. But this idea is wrong on both acounts. Your greatest potential for getting published is with the smaller-sized presses. This is the second major key to getting published!

The publishing company I am involved with is known as an independent, or small press. Small presses are companies that publish fewer than about ten or so *new* books each year, although some companies which publish as many as 30 books a year may also call themselves small presses. These companies can be little Mom and Pop operations, or modest-sized corporations with several dozen employees. Many two- or three-person operations have been very successful, and through the years have grown into substantial corporations.

Although small presses don't publish as many books as large companies do, there are many more small presses to work with. One-third of the publishing companies in operation today started less than ten years ago. Most of these would be considered small presses.

The smaller publishing companies are much more receptive to new authors. While the large companies will snub most unpublished authors, small publishers will be very receptive and willing to work with any writer who has a publishable manuscript. Small presses are your friend. Very few require submissions be sent in by agents. They are happy and willing to work directly with authors. They receive fewer submissions and aren't as discriminating about material that doesn't exactly fit the formal submission format. They are more willing to judge a manuscript by its merits, rather than by the way it was submitted. They, too, have learned by experience that a careless author usually produces unpublishable material, but they are more willing to work with an author who needs a little help polishing a manuscript, thus turning a work that might have been rejected elsewhere into a marketable book.

Even though small presses will be more receptive to books with limited customer appeal and will give new authors a chance, they are not pushovers. In general, they publish quality books equal in construction and content to those of the large companies. A poorly written manuscript will not be published by a small press any more than by a big New York company. They expect authors to show respect and send a professional submission and will be prejudiced against sloppy or careless work just like any publisher.

LARGE VERSUS SMALL PUBLISHING COMPANIES

Working with New Writers

There are many advantages to the small or independent press over the larger companies. The smaller companies are more receptive to and more tolerant of new authors. Most do not require agents. They are more willing to spend time and to work with someone who has a good book idea, but who may need a little help preparing and developing it into a marketable product.

If I get a submission that fits in with the rest of our books, is on a subject I feel is needed, and can be successfully marketed to our type of customers, I am very willing to work with the author, even though the material may need a lot of editorial work. An incomplete or poorly written manuscript is pretty much useless. But, if the author has an interesting idea, is an authority on the subject, and has at least average writing skills, I will be willing to work with the individual. It will take more of my time than most other materials, require more editing, and perhaps some rewriting, but I am willing to put forth this effort if I see potential in the book. The same book may not receive any attention from a large or medium-sized company. Editors with these companies deal with so many submissions from authors and agents that they can't take the time to develop submissions which may need a little extra work. I am busy too, but I am willing to devote time to a potentially good book, even though the author may not be a polished writer.

The big publishers prefer that new writers hone their skills by working with smaller presses, magazines, and newspapers before approaching them. So, the small press provides a service to budding writers who need experience. Very few writers ever sell their first book or magazine article. It usually takes several years before a writer develops the skill to be able to sell his or her writing consistently. Most first sales are to small companies.

Financial Considerations

So small publishers may be more receptive to new authors, but can they sell enough books to make it worth your time? Won't a large company be able to sell more copies of your book? After all, they have more money to spend on advertising and marketing.

The answer to these questions may surprise you. As a new and unknown author you have the potential to make more money going with a small publisher than you do with a big one.

Small publishing companies have smaller staffs, lower overhead expenses, and are usually run more efficiently. For these reasons, a small press can make a profit selling fewer books than the large or medium-sized companies. This is very important to you as an author.

Small presses do not need, or necessarily even look for, the potential bestseller. They can make a profit by selling books that would be unprofitable to the large publishers. This does not mean that small presses don't have bestsellers, as many of them do, but simply that their existence does not rely on them.

As I have shown, the large publishers need to sell at least 5,000 copies of most of their books before they prove profitable enough to reprint. Small publishers, on the other hand, can make a profit selling 2,000 or 3,000 books, or even less. Suppose you sell a book to a large publisher and, like 80 percent of all the other books published, it goes out of print after the first printing. Let's say the publisher eventually sold all 5,000 copies. You would be paid a royalty on a total of 5,000 books and that's it. Now, if you had sold the book to a small press, and considering they probably don't have all the advertising money and marketing muscle the big publisher has, could only sell 3,000 copies the first year. The small press would consider the book a success. They would reprint the book and sell another 3,000 the next year, and the next, and the next. They might keep the book in print for 20 years or more. That's a total of 60,000 books! The small press would have paid you a royalty on the sale of 60,000 books, compared to only 5,000 by the large publisher. Typically, a book's biggest sales occur within the first year it is released. After that, sales usually taper off. But even then, if the book only lasted three or four years, you would still make more money with the small press than you would with the larger company. I know from experience with my own company that many of the books we're still publishing and selling,, if published by a larger company would have been taken out of print years ago. Having a book in print 10 or 20 years is not uncommon. Small presses like to keep their books in print as long as possible, and with occasional updates and new editions, most books can have a life expectancy of decades.

Marketing and Promotion

What do a calorie conscious cookbook, a steamy romance novel, an exotic travel guide, and a children's picture book have in common? Nothing. Yet large publishing companies will promote and sell them in the same way to the same markets. Because these publishers produce so many books, they are compelled to handle them all in much the same way—marketing primarily to bookstores.

Although bookstores are good places to sell many general interest books, not all books sell well there because not all types of people shop there. Romance novels do not sell to the same type of people who buy auto repair manuals, but they are marketed and sold together. A more effective strategy for marketing many books would be to target each one to a specific type of buyer—a children's picture book to a toy store, or a gardening book to a nursery, for instance. However, the majority of books will never reach these markets.

Many potential book buyers do not visit bookstores. Small publishing companies recognize this fact and aggressively pursue alternative markets. In fact, non-bookstores are the primary sales outlet for many small companies. While a regional guidebook's sales may waver in a bookstore, it may be a popular seller in a tourist shop. Likewise, the best outlets for many books are not in bookstores. For this reason, small publishers can compete with their larger counterparts, and can even be more successful.

Most small presses specialize in only a few subjects. Many concentrate on a single topic which may be very broad like health and fitness, or more defined like antique doll collecting. They become experts in their fields of publication. They know what can sell and to whom they can sell it. In fact, they can do a much better job selling books in their specialty than the big publishers can, even though they have fewer resources and less financial and promotional muscle. They have a keener sense of the market, and are willing to spend the time promoting books that large publishers could not sell as effectively. To give you an example, Architectural Book Publishing Company is a successful small publishing company. They publish books on architecture and industrial arts. They know how to market their books and have established distribution channels. They do not limit the sale of their books to just bookstores, but sell to schools, city and state governments, and other non-bookstore outlets.

Another small company is High Text, which publishes books dealing with electronics and related subjects. They reprinted two books that were originally published by McGraw-Hill and Prentice Hall—two of the industry's largest companies. One of the books was on integrated circuit applications and the other was on shortwave radio listening. The original publishers sold the books only through their normal retail book channels. After mediocre sales, both books were taken out of print. When High Text reprinted the books, they largely ignored the traditional book markets and focused their efforts on electronics parts dealers, shortwave radio distributors, and mail order catalogs for radio and electronics enthusiasts. In less than one year High Text was able to sell more copies of both books than McGraw-Hill and Prentice Hall were able to in over three years! Because of their flexibility, aggressiveness, and marketing knowledge, small publishing companies can be more successful with books within their specialty.

A question you might ask is: if a big company has more money to spend on advertising and promotion, can't they advertise their books to bring people into the bookstores? Experience has shown that most types of advertising for books is not cost-effective. Advertising is not directed toward persuading the public to rush down to their nearest bookstore to buy some new book, because this doesn't work. Most advertising is directed to book buyers to inform them that a new book by a favorite author or celebrity is out.

Publishers focus on other promotional methods to publicize their books: book reviews, author signings, and talk show appearances, to name a few. Other than a few select titles, no book gets the promotion it deserves.

The truth is that large publishers will spend very little time or money promoting most of their books. The vast majority of their advertising and publicity dollars go toward promoting a handful of their most promising bestsellers. The rest of their books get little more exposure than being mentioned in their general catalog.

As I explained earlier in this chapter, production and overhead expenses must be taken out of the publisher's revenues first. This leaves about five percent for advertising and profit. With limited capital available, publishers channel most of their advertising dollars into actively promoting only a small number of their books. They can't promote every book as they should because doing so would eat into their already narrow profit margin.

With a small publishing company, overhead expenses are smaller, and other expenses are carefully monitored to reduce waste. This gives the small publisher a larger profit margin and allows him to give each book individual attention and some degree of promotion and publicity. Even though smaller companies may not spend much on advertising, the money they do spend is targeted to the most receptive markets. They invest much more time and effort promoting each of their books than a big company would, simply because each book has a greater bearing on the company's overall success.

The Bestseller

At this point you might be thinking, "Sure, for most books maybe it would be best to go with a small press, but what about authors who have potential bestsellers? I just *know* my book will sell well, I can feel it." (According to the query letters I get from authors, it seems most of them believe they have written the next bestseller. This is especially true for unpublished writers.) If you do have a potential bestseller, won't a big publisher be more successful with it?

Conceivably, a large publisher would be able to promote a potential bestseller more effectively, and initially would probably sell more copies of the book. Big publishing companies do have an advantage in that they have well-established marketing systems and the money to promote and advertise hot-selling products much better than their smaller competitors. However, in the long run the differences are often minimal.

A small press can still have a book reach bestseller status. Any company that is established enough to be listed in *Writer's Market* or *Literary Market Place* should have the marketing contacts and ability to service almost every bookstore in the country.

Let me give you an example. There was a first-time author who wrote a military-suspense novel. Like most novice writers, he approached the big New York publishing companies, but his novel was rejected. He then sent it to what was, at the time, a small, relatively obscure publishing company called Naval Institute Press. They readily accepted his manuscript and produced the book *The Hunt for Red October* by Tom Clancy. The book became a national bestseller and eventually was made into a major motion picture starring Sean Connery. When sales of the book started to skyrocket, the publisher, knowing it had a successful book on its hands, sold the publishing rights to The Berkley Publishing Group, one of the large New York publishing houses. Berkley then used all of its marketing and advertising resources to promote and sell the book. In the end, the book sold (and still is selling) to all the places it would have sold if it had been originally published by a big publisher. The author became famous and very wealthy. It did not matter that a small press initially published the book. Clancy received just as much recognition and just about as much revenue by going with the small press as he would have if a big company had been the original publisher.

My conclusion is that you will be more successful in getting published and probably earn more money by going with a small publishing company instead of a larger one. This is the second key to publishing success.

You do not see this information mentioned in most other books on getting published. Why? Maybe because most other books on the subject are produced by big publishing companies and, therefore, are written from their perspective. This is not what new writers need. New writers need to know the realities of publishing, not just what is expected by the large presses.

Disadvantages of a Small Press

Are there any disadvantages to getting published by a small press? Well, there are some things you should be aware of. Because these companies are small, they are more likely to be adversely influenced by economic conditions. They could go out of business at any time. Large companies could too, but are usually a bit more stable. Although large companies are frequently gobbled up by larger ones and cease to exist as separate firms, the chances of a large publishing company folding is probably less.

With some caution, you can greatly reduce the chances of working with a company that will unexpectedly go bankrupt. First, choose companies that produce at least three new titles each year. Companies that produce fewer than this are probably too small to be of much benefit to you. They have limited resources, shallow marketing networks, and are highly susceptible to economic conditions. Choose a strong company, which can be determined by the number of new books they publish each year and by the length of time they have been in business. If the company has been around for 10 years or so, they apparently know what they are doing and have an established marketing network. Be very cautious with any small press that has been in existence less than three years. Information on the number of books published, length of time in business, as well as many other important aspects of the company can be found in *Writer's Market* and other directories. The publishers of *Writer's Market* and *Literary Market Place* screen the companies to some extent, listing in their book publishers section only those who produce at least three or more new titles each year. This isn't a guarantee the company is stable or effective, but it eliminates thousands of the very small publishers or non-publishing companies who only publish on the side.

The number of new books a publisher publishes each year can give you a rough idea of the size of the company. Although I have indicated that a small press usually publishes 10 books or fewer a year, there is no real benchmark. When a publishing house starts producing more than 30 or 40 new books a year, it begins to approach the business of publishing with the same prejudices and attitudes as the publishing giants, and your chances of seeing your work published by them diminish. Those who produce fewer than 20 or 30 books per year will be your best bet. Your chances of publication improve as the companies get smaller.

The primary disadvantage with small presses is that they generally offer smaller advances. Some don't offer an advance at all. There is nothing wrong with this. An advance is always a payment against royalties, that is, money paid to the author before the book has earned any. It is not extra income paid in addition to the royalties. It is part of the royalties that your book is expected to earn. You have no doubt heard of authors who were offered six-figure advances. You hear about these only because they are rare, and are only offered by the publishing giants who have the financial resources to do so. Advances rarely exceed what the publisher expects the book to earn back in one year—that is, the number of copies the publisher expects to sell in the first year, multiplied by the royalty per copy. Most advances are generally in the $1,000 to $5,000 range. Small companies may only offer a few hundred dollars, if anything at all. If your book sells as expected, you will receive the same amount, regardless of the size of the advance.

However, most books do not sell as well as the author or publisher had hoped. Advances are usually nonrefundable. So, if a book does not sell well enough to compensate the publisher for the author's advance, the publisher suffers the loss. The author comes out ahead by receiving a larger royalty payment than the sales of his or her book warranted. Since most books (80 percent) published by the big publishers are not reprinted, agents try to get the biggest advance possible. They know that in many cases the advance will be bigger than the actual amount the book will earn.

Small presses aren't affected as much by books that don't sell well, as their success ratio is much greater than 20 percent. For instance, the company I am associated with, which is a small press, has a 70 percent *success* rate. Seven out of every 10 books we publish are reprinted. It may take us twice as long to sell some of our books as compared to a larger publisher, but we keep the books in print, and reprint them over and over again. But some books do go out of print, and it is almost impossible to predict which ones will. So, an author is usually better off getting as big an advance as possible, regardless who publishes the book. But the fact that you may not get a big advance should not deter you from working with a small press.

It is important to keep in mind, particularly when working with small publishers, the types of books they publish. Small publishers are successful because they specialize in only a few subject areas. They can even be more effective selling books in these areas than the publishing giants because they know the market better.

For general interest books a large company will probably sell more per year than a small press can. But small presses will keep their books in print much longer, earning the author greater royalties. For specialized subjects small presses are frequently much more successful than the big publishers.

If a small publisher has several other books on the same subject as yours, he will probably do a good job of marketing it. If, on the other hand, your book is unlike any of the others he produces, you should be cautious. If he is not strong in your book's subject area, he will have to open new markets and devise new advertising and promotional strategies. This is expensive and, for a single book, usually not profitable. If he is trying to break into a new market and your book is one of several he is introducing, that is okay. But if your book will be the only one of its kind produced by that publisher, be very cautious. It is not likely that he will have the financial muscle or the experience to effectively market a single book out of his area of expertise.

In this chapter I have focused most of my comments on book publishers, but the same basic idea applies to magazine publishers. If you want to get an article published, your best chances will be with a small press. I discuss magazines in some detail in the next chapter.

CHAPTER 5

WRITING AND SELLING MAGAZINE ARTICLES

Whether you are primarily interested in writing magazine articles or books, this chapter will be of interest to you. Article writing is a great training ground for good writing. If you want to learn to become a good writer, you need to write. Through article writing you have the opportunity to improve your skills and get feedback from people in the publishing industry.

There are literally thousands of magazines, newspapers, newsletters, and other periodicals covering an enormously wide range of interests. This provides writers bountiful opportunities for publication. One of the best ways of becoming a published author is by writing articles for periodicals. Good writing skills and a good topic are still required, but the time and effort needed to produce an article and see it in print is much less than it is for a book. You can get a response from magazine editors quicker and work on many more ideas. You could waste years writing a book that has no commercial value, but if one article idea is rejected you can quickly try others until you find one that interests an editor.

There are a large number of periodicals, ranging from the purely scientific to the association newsletters to general interest tabloids. The type of writing and skill required for each varies. Some publications are very selective, all submissions must be very well-written and follow their publishing guidelines. Some editors will reject a manuscript if a couple of grammar or spelling errors are found. On the other hand, there are many small publications which welcome almost any relevant topic regardless of the author's literary skill. The popular newsstand magazines are very selective, and consequently pay the best. Lesser-known publications pay very little or nothing at all. The big advantage of having an article published by these smaller publications is that it provides you with experience and gives you publishing credits. Any publisher, whether book or magazine, will look more favorably upon an author who has publishing credits with legitimate publications, regardless of the amount that may have been paid. The fact that a publication had enough confidence in your work to publish it indicates some degree of competence. However, the more prestigious the publication the better. An editor will be more impressed by an author who has been published in *Time, Good Housekeeping,* or *Sports Illustrated* than in *Beekeeping Monthly* or some other obscure publication. Why? Because the requirements for publication in the high-profile consumer magazines are more strict. Still credits from lesser-known publications are valuable. You can develop good writing skills and publishing credits by writing for these smaller publications.

As a publisher, I am much more impressed by an author who has had several articles published by small publications than one who has had nothing published.

Don't claim to be a published author unless you can back up your statements. Give the names of the publications, at least. You may also provide other details, such as title and date of the article. A copy of the article is also beneficial, for it provides verification of your claim and gives the editor a sample of your writing skill. I get queries all the time from people who claim to be published authors but fail to mention who published their work or what type of material it was. Making such a claim without verification does the author more harm than good. Why?

Because many authors who make unsubstantiated claims often don't know how to properly submit a query or their writing skill is obviously below par. When people state that they are published authors, but do not back it up, I assume either that the publication is some local newsletter or church bulletin, or the author is simply lying. Either way, it gives me a bad impression of the author and I am immediately prejudiced against his or her material. So, if you can't back up your claim of being a published author, don't mention it! If your list of publications is long, just mention a few of the most prestigious or include a list on a separate sheet of paper.

I like receiving sample articles or clips from authors because it proves they have been published, it gives me an idea of their writing ability, and it shows that they have confidence in their work. When sending clips or tearsheets, send articles on subjects of a similar topic or nature to the one you are proposing. If you are proposing a humorous book or article, send a clip from a previous humorous article you have had published. If you want to write an interview, send an interview; a how-to, send a how-to (preferably on a similar subject). This way the editor will have an idea of your writing style and ability in regards to the proposed topic.

Send no more than three appropriate clips. You do not need to overwhelm the editor with your writing credits. Send the complete article and write the name of the publisher and publication date on the piece.

CONSUMER AND TRADE PUBLICATIONS

There are two major types of periodicals: consumer magazines and trade publications. Consumer magazines are purchased in newsstands or by subscription. They can be general interest publications such as *Reader's Digest* and *Life,* or slanted toward a special interest, such as *Sports Afield*, *Seventeen*, and *Mature Living*. Articles in these publications are meant to inform and entertain. The trade journal or newsletter, on the other hand, is the voice of an industry or an association. Information contained in them has to be detailed and specific.

Writer's Market contains an extensive listing of consumer and trade publications. A sample of the various types of publications listed includes: *The Lawyer's Word, Coal People Magazine, Golf Shop Operations, Print & Graphics, Juggler's World,* and *Pet Age.* Although *Writer's Market* includes over 3,000 periodicals, it only lists publications which are actively looking for freelance submissions. There are thousands of small publications which are not listed that also accept some freelance submissions. Many associations and other organizations publish magazines and newsletters and welcome freelance submissions, although they frequently do not offer the author payment, except perhaps in the form of a few copies of the publication. These are still legitimate publications that will provide good writing experience and credit. No matter what your interests are, you are bound to find publications devoted to them.

How do you track down trade publications which may not be listed in *Writer's Market*? An extensive list of associations, many of which publish newsletters for their members, can be found in the *Encyclopedia of Associations.* You can find a copy of this directory in your library.

SMALL PUBLICATIONS

New writers often make the mistake of trying to sell only to the largest and most popular magazines. These magazines receive thousands of submissions every month, but buy only a very few. Your chances of breaking into print with one of these giants are extremely small. *Redbook,* for example, receives 3,000 short story submissions monthly, but publishes only two or three of them in each issue. Your chances of selling a manuscript to them is one in 1,000! Obviously, not very good odds. However, if you go to a much smaller publication such as *Flipside,* which receives five to six submissions a month and publishes six to eight a year, your chances increase to one in ten. For this reason alone it is generally much easier to get into print with the smaller publications.

Many of the smaller publications are hungry for material and will accept almost any article for publication that is targeted toward the publication's readership. Any budding writer should be able to get published somewhere. Getting published in these small publications is a stepping stone. As you gain more experience and your writing skills improve, you can approach the more prestigious publications with a greater probability of success.

Payment for articles varies widely from publication to publication. The popular consumer magazines with large circulations will pay anywhere from $1,000 to $5,000 for feature articles. This is a major reason why they are swamped with submissions and why competition is so fierce. More typically you can expect payment of around $200 or $300 from most modest-sized publications.

Some of the smaller publications and technical journals frequently pay with a free subscription or a few sample copies of the issue which contains your article. Many small publications don't offer anything other than to include your byline, and you may even have to purchase the issue to get a copy of your printed article. This doesn't mean these publications are not respected or that getting published in them is worthless—it's not. You will gain experience and a publishing credit that you can use as a reference in future query letters.

Admittedly, it is more impressive to an editor if you have been published in a major consumer magazine, but for a beginner that is almost impossible. Start with the smaller publications and work your way up. Don't try to start at the top, competing with seasoned professionals. These people have been perfecting their writing talents for decades. Take your time, develop your writing skills, and earn writing credits from the small presses first. It's better to sell an article to a small magazine and receive only $50 than it is to not make a sale to a large magazine.

SELLING TO MAGAZINES

Usually new writers approach the magazine market by writing an article on a subject of interest to them, and then go around searching for a publisher, much like you would do for a book. However, most successful freelance writers do not recommend this. Although many small publications will readily accept and publish unsolicited manuscripts, most consumer and trade publications will not.

Like book publishers, magazine publishers are besieged with submissions. Because they have so much material available to them, they are highly selective. For this reason your chances of getting an unsolicited manuscript published are remote. Whether you contact a small or large publication, always send publishers a query letter first, even before you write the article. How to write and submit query letters will be discussed in detail in the next chapter.

The following five steps are used by most successful writers to get their articles published. Preparing your material like a professional will give you the best opportunity for publication.

Step One

Choose a general subject which is of interest to you. This should be a subject you would enjoy studying and writing about. A saying commonly repeated by editors is "write what you know." This is good advice. Pick a subject you know about or would like to learn about. The more you know about a particular subject and the more you are interested in the subject, the better job you will do writing about it. Many first time authors write on a subject they are very familiar with and are successfully published. With encouragement from their first successful publication, they attempt to write on other topics which they are less experienced with, but fail to interest editors and wonder why. A piece on "Real Estate Investment in Rural Areas" might be right for some publication, but if you don't know anything about real estate and don't care much about it, you probably shouldn't even try to write such an article. The best writing is produced by enthusiastic writers. If you can't get enthused about a topic, it will show in your writing and will probably be unsaleable.

Step Two

Read and study your chosen topic. If you have an interest in a particular area, you probably already have subscriptions to magazines on the topic. If not, subscribe to them or go to the library and read them. Use *Writer's Market* and other reference sources to make a list of all publications within your particular subject. As you read, look for popular trends, controversies, and subjects which appear to be of most interest.

Step Three

Choose a specific topic to write about. Ideas will come to you as you read about your chosen subject. Do some preliminary research on your chosen topic to determine if you can find enough material to write a saleable article. Make an outline of your proposed article to see if you can adequately develop and write it. Do not write the article yet.

Step Four

Write a query letter describing your article idea and state your qualifications (writing credits, experience, training, etc.). Keep the letter to no more than one page if possible. Address your letter to the proper editor by name. Names can be found in *Writer's Market* or in the masthead of the magazine. A letter addressed to simply "Editor" is a sure sign of an amateur. You may give an estimated time for completion of the article. Spend some time composing your letter and reread it to eliminate any spelling or grammatical errors. Submit your query to every publication on the list you previously made. Wait for a response. If you send the queries out together, let the editor know that it is a simultaneous submission. Check with *Writer's Market* first as some publications dislike multiple submissions.

Allow about six weeks for all publishers to respond. If some of the publications do not respond to your initial mailing, resubmit your query and mention that this is a follow-up letter. Always include a stamped self-addressed envelope for a response.

Step Five

If one of the publications accepts your idea and assigns you to write the article, you've been successful. You then write the article and submit it. If you sent out multiple submissions and more than one publication is interested in your article, choose the one that makes the best offer.

What happens if none of the publications initially accept your article idea? You don't have to throw away your idea and start all over again at step one. Keep your original topic but change it slightly by giving it a new focus or new slant, and resubmit it to all of the publications on your list. Keep revising and resubmitting until you make a sale.

Let me give you an example. Let's say you chose hunting and fishing as your general topic of interest. You've made a list of all publications that print articles related to hunting and fishing and studied the articles in them. You chose a specific topic such as "Bass Fishing on the Yellowstone River." Submit query letters to the publications on your list. If all of them reject your initial proposal, revise your topic slightly to something such as "Trout Fishing on the Yellowstone River" and try again. Keep trying until you sell the article. You may eventually end up writing an article titled "Fishing for Shark off the Alaskan Coast," but you will make the sale. This is the process most professionals use. It saves time and gets results.

Study the Markets

You wouldn't necessarily send the same query letter to every editor. Slant the letter to interest the editor and the publication's readers.

The primary reason most article ideas are rejected by editors is because the writer did not take the time to study the magazine's needs. The articles are not in harmony with the magazine's focus and readership.

Every publication is different. Each looks for a particular voice, style, and viewpoint. Even two similar magazines could have very different readerships. For example, two magazines on health and fitness could cater to different age groups, one for young audiences and the other for more mature readers, or they could cater to different income levels or attitudes. Although articles in the two publications may be similar in concept, they could have a distinctly different focus. You need to become familiar enough with the publications you submit material to, so you can slant your articles to the readers' interests. In order to do this, you will need to study the publications before submitting anything to them. By studying them, I don't just mean reading the articles. You need to carefully examine the entire publication to get a clear idea of the type of people who read it.

The most obvious way of determining the magazine's focus is by analyzing the cover. The cover design and featured articles advertise the magazine's image and will give you an idea of the types of people who read it. The next most important element you should look at are the featured articles. Try to determine the interests and personalities of the people for whom they were written.

Don't restrict your reading to just the articles; read the editorials and other material. Make a point of reading the editor's column, letters to the editor, and any special short features. These will contain valuable insights into the character of the readership. Also, you should study the ads. Since advertisers pay a pretty penny to advertise, they carefully choose the publications they advertise in. What type of products or services are advertised? What can you say about the kinds of people who would buy these products and services? A magazine that carries ads depicting families and children would suggest a readership interested in family unity and concerned about the family issues. These are the type of people for whom you would be writing your article.

As you study the publications, ask yourself which specific topics seem to interest the magazine's editors. Which topics seem to get the most coverage? What trends are currently hot?

What controversies, problems, and viewpoints stir up the most interest? The letters to the editor section is a gold mine for this type of information. As you study, use your imagination and seek intriguing topics which would be of interest to the magazine's readers.

Slant your query letter to each magazine rather than sending the same letter to all. Emphasize points you believe coincide with the focus of the publication. When you write the article, slant your material to that viewpoint. If the editor believes that the article is not written with the right viewpoint, it could still be rejected.

Don't send a 10,000-word article to a magazine that never publishes anything larger than 2,000 words. Learn what size articles are appropriate for the magazine you are interested in and write your articles within those limits. Most magazine editors will give you a word limit. This isn't just a recommendation; it is a requirement you must follow closely. If you add more, they will cut something out. If your article falls short, they may come back and ask you to write more. Stay as close to the requested length as possible. Magazines have a precise amount of space to fill and all articles must fit the available space.

Unsolicited Manuscripts

Although I have told you that it is preferable to send query letters before writing the article, you may know of authors who have not done this or who have even had unsolicited manuscripts published. Most freelance writers and magazine editors recommend that writers send query letters first and then write the article, but it isn't always necessary. Let me mention a couple of exceptions.

Many professional writers write their articles first and have been successful in getting them published. However, those who have had success with this method have been writing and perfecting their skills for many years. They know their markets and slant their work toward each magazine's interests and viewpoints. Also, having an impressive list of writing credits will spark an editor's interest. Editors can tell if a submission is from a professional by the way it is written and from the information it contains. However, unless you are an experienced writer with many writing credits, it is best that you follow the advice of the professionals and query first and then write the article.

There is one more exception. While most publications will generally not read unsolicited manuscripts, many of the smaller ones will. You can approach small publications directly with a cover letter and your manuscript. These companies are much more receptive to unpublished authors and much more willing to examine unsolicited material. If your work is of interest to the magazine's readership and you have provided useful information written in a readable (not necessarily exquisite or flawless) manner, it has a very good chance of being published. Many small publications are hungry for good, useful articles.

Short Stories

Unlike magazine articles, most publications that buy short stories prefer to receive the entire story with the author's initial contact. They would just as soon read the story as read a synopsis or author's bio. Some don't necessarily even want a cover letter. I think a cover letter is useful if it is brief. Simply state the type of story you have and let the story sell itself. If you have had previous contact with the editor, you might want to mention that, too.

Some publications prefer writers to submit query letters before sending short stories, just as you would a magazine article. They want to be sure your story is slanted towards their audience. Every magazine has a style or viewpoint that characterizes everything it publishes. If the proposed story isn't in complete harmony with the magazine's character, it won't be published.

You need to write your story with a particular magazine and audience in mind. Let the magazine's needs be your guide as you develop your characters, plot, and dialog. Slant your story to the reader's interests and don't use anything that doesn't fit the magazine's character.

Look in *Novel and Short Story Writer's Market* for publications interested in publishing short stories. This reference lists book and magazine publishers interested in receiving fiction. It's published by the same people who put out *Writer's Market* and follows the same format. In it you can find out who to send queries to, what type of material each publisher is looking for, and other useful information regarding writing and submitting short stories.

WORKING WITH MAGAZINE EDITORS

If the editor thinks your idea has some promise but you are an inexperienced writer, he may ask you to write the article or a portion of it on speculation, that is, without a promise to buy the finished article. That way he can see how well you do. He may also ask you for an outline of the proposed article before he'll actually give you the go-ahead to write it.

You should make a basic outline of your proposed article before you write the query letter. Your initial research lays the foundation of the information you would include, and how you would structure the article. Using your original outline as a guide, you could write a new outline geared specifically to any publication which shows interest in your article idea.

The outline should be double-spaced and limited to about two or three pages. In the outline tell precisely how the article will be structured, how you will approach the subject, what people you plan to interview (if any), what research or studies you will use, etc.

Editors want to know how much thought you have put into your article idea. Having a detailed outline shows them that you have done some initial research and can complete the article. This is what editors want to see. If you are new to the editor, whether you've been published or not, the editor will want to know if you are capable of writing an acceptable article. If he doesn't request an outline from an unknown writer, how is he to know if the author is capable of writing a satisfactory story?

Many aspiring magazine writers have come to editors with great story ideas and received the assignment to write the article only to find that writing it was not as easy as expected, and, consequently, the article died. This is a waste of time for an already busy editor and creates problems in scheduling articles for the publication. Your outline shows the editor you know what you're doing and can do the job.

If you get an assignment to write your proposed article, you should work within the limits the editor gives. These limits may include article length, submission deadline, and suggestions on how to present the information. When you send in your article, include a cover letter briefly explaining the article and reminding him of previous correspondence. In the time you spent writing the article, the editor may have talked to literally hundreds of other writers about their material, and you or your assignment may not be immediately remembered.

After your manuscript has been submitted to the editor it will go through an editing process. The editor will make corrections, additions, deletions, and changes as he sees fit. He may do some extensive rewriting if he feels it is necessary, or he may return it to you to rewrite. If serious changes are considered necessary, the editor will usually consult with you about a revision. A good editor will only make changes when absolutely necessary. You've got to trust the editor. The changes he suggests or makes are based on his experience and knowledge of the magazine and its readers.

Some of the larger publications will send you a galley proof of your article to check before publication. Most, however, will not. The galley is beneficial, as it will show you what editing changes were made to your article before publication. If you have concerns, spot errors, or have a problem with how your article was edited, you can talk to the editor. Although the editor has the right to make the final decision as to what gets published, if you have serious concerns, something can generally be worked out between you. At least you will understand the reasons for the editor's changes.

After sending the editor your manuscript, you may not hear back from him until after the article has been published. By then it is obviously too late to make changes and you will have to live with the editor's decisions. Usually this does not cause a problem; however, sometimes you may be annoyed at having something changed. There's not much you can do about it. At any rate, unless the editor made some serious errors in the editing process, it is best not to complain. After all, his job is to edit the material he buys and he has that right.

Sometimes after you have written and submitted the article, the editor will reject it. Just because the publication gave you the go-ahead to write the article does not necessarily mean they will publish it, or that you will get paid the stated fee. The completed article will still have to be reviewed and accepted. If the article is well-written and fits their needs, chances are it will be published. However, any number of things can occur that will prevent the article from being published. The primary reason is that the author simply could not present the material in a satisfactory manner to the editor. If the editor is still interested in using the article he will have the author make revisions. Sometimes he will cancel the assignment. Another reason for not publishing the article is that the editor decides the subject is no longer of interest. Some topics may be of interest one day, but not a few months later. Even in the short time it takes to write the article, the readers' interests may have changed. Current events and trends change at an unpredictable pace. Another reason for non-publication is that a competitor may have recently printed a very similar article.

If your article is canceled you will normally receive a kill fee, which is a percentage of the original amount promised (typically about 20 percent). This is a sum paid by the publication to compensate you for your time in writing the article.

Even if your article is accepted and paid for, it still may not be printed. Oh sure, you've got the money, but you miss out on seeing your work in print and being able to use it as a writing credit because it wasn't actually used. This happens to mayb, as many as 10 percent of the articles accepted. Most magazines have a set limit of pages, and the amount of article space is determined by the amount of advertising space sold.

Since magazines make the majority of their profit from advertising, ad copy gets priority over articles. For this reason some articles will inevitably be delayed or even cut entirely. Some articles, which are not particularly timely, can be held for years before they are published. I've heard of writers who have had articles appear in print as long as four years after submission.

A more agonizing experience is to have the article accepted, but with terms of pay-on-publication. This means the author will be paid the amount offered when the article is actually published. Many articles accepted under such terms of payment are delayed or never printed for one reason or another. In the latter case, not only do you not get into print but you don't get paid either. Often the article ages (becomes outdated) so it is unsaleable to other publications.

Many publications pay only on publication. You might be able to negotiate for payment on acceptance. If you are a relatively inexperienced writer, the publisher may not be easily persuaded to modify his offer. If you are a published author and have proven your ability to get published, you have more leverage to work with when negotiating with a publisher, and can more readily find another publisher if necessary.

SELLING RIGHTS TO YOUR WRITING

Whenever you sell an article to a publication you are really selling rights to the work. There are several different types of rights recognized by the law that you can sell. Normally, if no specific rights were mentioned when a publication offers to buy your article, the law states that the publication is buying only *one-time rights* to the work. This means the author still retains ownership of the copyright and can resell the same piece to other publications. The publication also has no guarantee that it will be the first to publish the article.

Most publications try to buy specific types of rights. A new writer may lose a sale if he or she does not agree to the rights requested by the publication. Experienced writers have more say in what rights they will sell and can negotiate with the publication. New writers are more willing to sell greater rights to their work and accept moderate payments just to break into print. Professional writers cannot afford to do this. They sell to the highest paying markets and retain as many rights as possible so that they can resell their work to other publications.

The rights most typically sold to publications are *first serial rights*. This is the right to publish the material for the first time in any publication. The writer retains all other rights.

A variation on first-serial rights is *first North American serial rights*. This means the buyer has the right to be the first one in North America to publish the work. Publications with distributions in both the U.S. and Canada prefer to buy these rights. If you sell only first North American serial rights, you are free to sell your work to publications outside of North America. These are called *foreign serial rights*.

Second serial rights give publications the right to reprint your work after it has been published elsewhere. Whether the work has been published once or many times, these rights are always referred to as second serial rights. This term is often used when a portion of a published book is reprinted as an article.

Publications which do not compete for the same audience will often buy *simultaneous rights* and print the work at about the same time. An example of this would be two religious publications—one aimed for Catholics and the other for Baptists. The topic of the article could be nondenominational and thus suitable for people of different religious faiths.

Syndication rights give a periodical the right to publish a series of excerpts from a book you have written. If the articles are published before the book is in print, you would be syndicating first serial rights to the book. If the book has already been published, you would be syndicating second serial rights.

Some magazines will want to purchase *all rights* to your work. Doing this gives the publication complete control of the material. You would not be able to resell the work in its present form. Those publications which buy all rights keep the material for use in other interests such as books and foreign markets. The payment to the author is usually higher, however.

Check with *Writer's Market* to see which rights the publications you approach usually request. On the first page of your manuscript, in the upper right hand corner, indicate the rights you are offering for sale. See the examples in Chapter 8.

TIPS ON ARTICLE WRITING

Choose a specific topic. "The Grand Canyon," for example, is such a broad topic that entire books can be written on it. Hundreds of articles can be written about various aspects of the Grand Canyon, all of which could have distinctly different markets. An article titled "Rock Climbing in the Grand Canyon" would appeal to people who subscribe to a rock climbing magazine, but would hardly be appropriate for a family oriented magazine. On the other hand, "Family Recreational Activities in the Grand Canyon" would be suitable. Other article topics such as "How to Get a Summer Job at the Grand Canyon" and "The Best Hiking Trails in the Grand Canyon" are examples of specific subjects that would appeal to different magazines.

For your article to be meaningful and saleable, you need to give it a direction or focus by adding a viewpoint or theme. What is the purpose of the article? What does the article accomplish? Make your overall message clear. If your article is titled "The Best Non-Alcoholic Party Drinks," your aim could be to provide exciting alternatives to alcohol and help the readers avoid the adverse effects of alcohol consumption. Your article should make readers think, and motivate them to take action. After reading about non-alcoholic drinks, readers should be excited about trying them at their next party or group gathering, or even just for fun with the family.

Viewpoint puts life into an article and makes it exciting and interesting. Without it the article is nothing more than a report. This may be all right for a technical journal, but not for most consumer magazines or even trade publications. Express your opinion and back it up with facts, personal experiences, and anecdotes which illustrate the points you make.

Include specific details and descriptions to illustrate and verify what you say. Don't just say the Grand Canyon is very deep. Tell exactly how deep it is and add colorful, personal descriptions. Don't just say, "Many people are killed by drunk drivers." Give facts and figures.

Organize your article. Make it follow a logical path from one point to the next. Connect different thoughts by smooth transitions, and remain on a single theme. Begin with a lead paragraph that will grab readers' interest. If the story starts out slow, few people will read it. Use a lead that will spark readers' interest and curiosity and involve them in reading your story. When writing your lead paragraph, however, don't use misleading statements or something irrelevant to the rest of your story.

Keep the story exciting; eliminate cliches, repetitive phrases, and extra words. Proofread it several times to catch spelling, grammar, and other errors. Make sure your facts are correct. If you follow all of these guidelines, you will be on the path to publication.

Let others read your articles and give you feedback. If there is a writers' group in your area, consider joining it. Practicing writing and getting feedback from others will help you improve your skills.

Some good books devoted entirely to writing articles include: *Breaking into Article Writing* by Sondra F. Enos, *How to Write and Sell Magazine Articles* by Shirley Biagi, *Write and Sell Your Free-Lance Article* by Linda Buchanan Allen, and *Writer's Digest Handbook of Magazine Article Writing* edited by Jean M. Fredette.

CHAPTER 6

QUERY LETTERS

In this chapter you will learn how to write and prepare effective query letters. Because query letters will be your initial contact with both book and magazine publishers, it is important that you prepare them properly and professionally.

USING QUERY LETTERS

A query is a letter you write to a publisher which requests a reading for your manuscript before you actually submit it. Publishers use query letters to screen potential submissions and invite only material which they would have an interest. Writing a good query letter is a vital step to getting published. Whether you are writing a book or a magazine article, your initial contact with the publisher should be a query letter.

Sometimes the query letter is sent by itself, sometimes as part of a submission packet which may include a synopsis, outline, or even the entire text. But in any submission, you must convince the editor that your material is worthy of consideration before the manuscript will be read.

If you want to sell a magazine article, initially send only a query letter. If you are trying to sell a book-length manuscript, most editors will prefer receiving a query first. Check with *Writer's Market* to find out exactly what each publisher wants. For the initial contact, some book publishers will want only a query letter, others want a query with a detailed book proposal, while some will accept a complete manuscript. No matter what material you send, you will need to include a query or cover letter. A cover letter will function as a query letter if it is your initial contact with the publisher and is sent with your book proposal or manuscript.

Sending a query letter first is actually better for both you and the publisher. You end up sending your manuscript to only those publishers who would have an interest in your material, thus saving you time, postage, and manuscript preparation costs and publishers aren't burdened with unsolicited and unwanted manuscripts.

A SELLING TOOL

When you send a query letter, you are, in essence, sending a sales letter to a business in an attempt to sell a product—your writing. You need to write a convincing letter that will interest and entice the editor to want to read your manuscript.

The query letter must be written in an interesting and compelling style. If you can't convince the editor to read your material, then it doesn't matter how good your manuscript is, it won't be read. Not only does the query tell the editor about your project, but it provides a sample of your writing ability and style. If your query letter is boring or difficult to read, it indicates that the manuscript will be of the same quality. A well-written query, on the other hand, suggests that you are capable of producing a publishable manuscript.

Don't try to be cute or funny. Hand-drawn cartoons and off-the-wall comments are juvenile. Publishing and writing is a business. Editors are professionals and expect those they work with to be the same.

Don't waste the editor's time by giving your opinion of how good your manuscript is and claiming that it will be a bestseller. An editor can tell much about your writing just from your letter and accompanying materials, and whether or not your subject has a chance in the market place. Making such claims makes you look naive and amateurish.

Appearance

The query letter is usually limited to one or two pages. It should be clean and neat, typed, not handwritten. Handwritten letters show a lack of professionalism. Since it is generally no longer than two pages, it should contain no typographical errors or obvious corrections. It must be grammatically correct and totally free of spelling errors. If you are using a typewriter and make a mistake, do not cross out the error and retype it or use correction fluid—retype the letter. Neatness does make an impression. If you do not care about the appearance of your query letter, the editor will assume that your manuscript will also be carelessly written and typed, and therefore will not invite you to submit it.

Format

Since the query letter is a business letter, it should be set up in a businesslike format. The letter should have your full name, address, phone number, and date. You should also include the name of the editor you are submitting to, the company name, and address. This information is found in directories like *Writer's Market.*

Most business letters use a block style format. Page 65 shows an example. You should type your name and address centered at the top of the sheet as shown. You might consider having some stationery printed with your name and address on it. Although printed stationery is not mandatory, it does help present yourself as a professional. When typing query letters or any business correspondence use the format illustrated.

Susan Wiley
132 Main Street
Alief, Texas, 77902
(713) 546-7483

July 12, 19—

Linda Roe
Submissions Editor
Healthy Living Magazine
101 Broadway
New York, NY 10011

Dear Ms. Roe:

Each year one million Americans are diagnosed as having cancer. As yet, there is no sure cure for this disease. Recent studies, however, by Prescott University and the American Cancer Foundation have demonstrated that certain nutrients in our food play a significant role in cancer prevention.

I would like to propose an article for you which explains the new breakthroughs that researchers have discovered in cancer prevention and how to benefit from them. The article would describe the types of foods which are high in cancer-fighting nutrients and how to prepare these foods to obtain the greatest nutritional value. Readers will also learn how to counter cancer-causing food additives, how to boost the body's immunity against cancer, and how hereditary factors leading to cancer can be overcome.

I am very familiar with the research being done in cancer prevention. Currently I am working on my Master of Science degree in biomedical technology at Prescott University and for the past two years have assisted in the cancer research. I have had articles published in *Prevention Magazine* and *Health and Fitness.*

I can have a 2,000-word article finished by August 30. If you would be interested in this article, please let me know. A self-addressed stamped envelope is enclosed for your convenience. This is a simultaneous query.

I look forward to your response.

Yours truly,
Susan Wiley
Susan Wiley

Sample of a query letter written in block style format.

Address

Submissions addressed to the "Fiction Editor," "Submissions Editor," "Editorial Director," or some other title are automatically returned or wind up in the slush pile—a pile of submissions which receive little or no attention. In order to avoid the initial round of rejections, you should address the letter to an editor by name. You can find names in directories such as *Writer's Market* or *Literary Market Place.* Editors are a highly mobile group and frequently jump from one company to another or change positions within a single company. Even though these directories are updated every year, as many as 25 percent of the listings in the current editions may be outdated. Some big publishing companies will return a submission unread if it is addressed to an editor who is no longer working there. To avoid this problem, you may want to call the company first and ask to whom you should send your query. This is more important with large companies than it is with the smaller ones. The editors at smaller companies are much more stable.

A letter addressed to a specific person will unquestionably receive more attention than one that is not. After all, if the sender knows the editor by name, the editor may have had previous dealings with the author or may have even requested the submission, so it will receive preferential treatment.

In the salutation of the letter, use Mr. or Ms., not the editor's first name. If gender cannot be determined, use the full name (e.g., Dear Leslie Smith). Once you have corresponded for a while you may begin your salutation with the editor's first name, but usually only after the editor begins calling you by your first name.

SIMULTANEOUS SUBMISSIONS

To save time and increase your chances for a positive response, you may contact several editors at the same time. This is referred to as a simultaneous submission. In the past, the standard practice was for an author to send submissions to only one publisher at a time. It took each publisher a month or more to evaluate the material and respond. Authors could only reach a few publishers a year. Since some manuscripts might be rejected by 20 or 30 publishers before being published, it could take years to find the right publisher. So, nowadays it has generaly become acceptable for authors to send out multiple submissions.

If you are sending out several query letters, let the editors know that you are making a simultaneous query. Although simultaneous submissions are acceptable to most publishers, some do not like them and will not consider any material submitted this way. Their reason is that they don't like the hassle of competing with other publishers. Check the individual listings in *Writer's Market* for those publishers who do not accept simultaneous submissions.

If two or more publishers do respond favorably to a simultaneous query and eventually offer to buy your manuscript, you have the option of making a choice. Select the one you feel will benefit you the most. If the publishers liked the material well enough, you may even get them to compete with each other. However, it is rare for publishers to want to invest much in a work from a new author, so they will probably not negotiate much. First-time authors have usually been rejected so often that when they get a positive response, they are happy to accept any offer. The possibility of losing the chance of getting published deters them from negotiating aggressively. If the author comes on too strong or is too demanding, the publisher may simply withdraw an offer to avoid dealing with a troublesome author.

Never use a form letter as a query, even if you are sending out multiple submissions. Although you may say the same thing in each letter, put the appropriate editor's name and address on each letter and sign them. Photocopied letters are unbusinesslike and almost always rejected.

HOW TO WRITE GOOD QUERY LETTERS

Good query letters will give the editors just enough information to describe your project and your qualifications, and convince them to read your manuscript. The basic elements for novel and magazine queries include: strong opening, description of the subject, author's qualifications, author's writing experience, availability of photographs, and closing. If you are writing a query for a nonfiction book you would also include promotional aids, potential market, and competition. Each of these topics are discussed below.

Opening

The opening is probably the most important part of your letter. You make your first impression by how you present yourself and describe your material. As the editor reads your letter she will be making judgments about you and your work. Start by explaining briefly what your book or article is about. Being overly descriptive or trying to be clever without getting directly to the point encourages a busy editor to skim your letter rather than read it.

If you are writing a novel, begin by giving the title of the book, its length, and the genre or category into which it falls (e.g., western, romance, science fiction, fantasy, mystery, etc.). You may mention that your book is in the same category as a particular well-known book. However, don't say that your manuscript is as good as, or better than, this book. Let the editor decide that on her own.

Here is an example of a simple, direct opening for a novel:

> I have just completed a 50,000-word science fiction novel entitled *Artificial Intelligence*. It is about an untested electronic brain that is transplanted into the skull of an accident victim.

This paragraph provides all the introductory information an editor needs to get an idea of the book and its category, and to make an initial judgment about the writer. No wasted words. No ravings about the merits or potential sales figures. Just straight-forward information. This is what editors like to see.

Like an intriguing novel with an enticing beginning, a strong opening will encourage the editor to read the rest of your letter with interest. We'll take a look at several examples.

> Over the past century no other college football rivalry has been as competitive, colorful, and nationally popular as the Army-Navy game. Since 1890, when the Midshipmen of the Naval Academy first challenged the Cadets of West Point, America's "service classic" has drawn the nation's attention (with competition so intense it once led to a duel between two officers, suspending the game for five years). I have written a 50,000-word book called *Army-Navy Football,* illustrating the rivalry between these two teams.

This is a good opening paragraph. Here are some other examples. The first one is for a book and the second one is for an article.

> The question of what to name the baby is often one of the biggest challenges faced by expectant parents, who usually respond by buying several books. I have written a book entitled *The Complete Guide to Baby Names* that goes far beyond the familiar standard and indiscriminate lists. It offers such complete support and guidance in this complex task that it is the only baby name book anyone will ever need.

> Every year the nonprofit community makes billions of dollars available to entrepreneurs, small-business owners, and people with ideas for profit-making ventures—often at rates as low as four

> percent! I propose to write a 3,000-word article outlining the steps necessary to find these funding sources and how to apply for financing. The article would explain where to look, the amount of money awarded, the number of grants or loans given, and a complete state-by-state listing of foundations and agencies to contact.

Citing interesting facts or statistics is one way you can create interest. See the following two examples—one on preventing foreclosure and the other on medical malpractice.

> Every month 50,000 people lose their homes through foreclosure. Many times this number are threatened with the loss of their homes as a result of illness, layoffs, or other financial problems. Since 1986 there have been more foreclosures per year than at any other time since the Great Depression. I have written a 45,000-word book designed to help financially troubled homeowners protect their homes from foreclosure.

> One out of every four doctors in America will be sued for malpractice during his or her career. Forty-three percent of all obstetricians and gynecologists in New York have been sued three or more times, and family doctors in rural areas have stopped delivering babies because they can't afford the premiums for the malpractice insurance. Of all the technologically developed countries, the United States is the only one with a malpractice crisis. We spend more money on health care per individual, but receive far less. I have written a book entitled *The Malpractice Crisis* which explores this crisis, its causes, implications, future impact, and what we can do about it.

Asking a few intriguing questions which are answered in your book or article may also induce an editor's interest.

> Why do horses stampede just before an earthquake? How can hawks swoop down on animals from distances we can't see even with high-powered binoculars? Or a snake find its prey in total darkness? Sight and hearing in the animal world go far beyond the somewhat limited range of sensory information humans possess. I have written a book titled *Animal Sense* which reveals the incredible physical adaptations that have evolved in the animal kingdom.

In some of the examples, the manuscript's title or length was not mentioned. This information need not always be stated in the opening paragraph. It may be placed in other parts of the letter if you desire. The point is to state briefly what the book or article is about in an interesting way that will encourage editors to want to read your letter and ultimately your manuscript.

Description of the Subject

The next paragraph or two can briefly outline the structure and content of the book or article. State some facts and mention people you intend to, or have, interviewed. Give the editor enough information to make him want to know more.

Here is an example of an opening paragraph and accompanying description of the manuscript:

> *Entrepreneur* magazine reports that 20 million Americans want to earn money in their spare time—everyone from housewives, retirees, and college students to full-time salaried employees. After reviewing over 2,000 spare-time opportunities, I have selected and compiled 100 of the best on the basis of profit potential, stability, reputation, and required start-up investment, into a book.
>
> My book, entitled *The 100 Best Spare-Time Opportunities.* features the best new dealerships,

> distributorships, license arrangements, and part-time investment ideas in America today—everything from selling pets at home parties to clowning. Readers don't have to be millionaires to benefit from any of these opportunities because each one can be launched for less than $1,000. Also included is a special profile on each opportunity—its market niche, growth potential, training, fees, and why it is considered a new top spare-time opportunity.

Here is another example:

> As a marriage and family counselor, I often ask my clients to read books with humorous, yet encouraging, messages. However, they can only read *All I Really Need to Know I Learned in Kindergarten* so many times. I recently confided to one client that I had nothing new to offer her, but that I would share some of my own notes with her instead. With some degree of sincerity she said, "You ought to publish those stories. They're funnier than the ones you've given to me to read, and they have a better message." Now you have to understand that she had just been released from a mental hospital only hours before.
>
> Needless to say, the idea made sense to me. Just as soon as she left, I sat down and began writing *I Was Born at an Early Age.* The book is a collection of humorous narratives with encouraging and helpful messages.
>
> The book describes life in Cut and Shoot, Texas, as seen through the eyes of a mischievous eight-year-old boy. A boy who grew up knowing George Bush's in-laws, Randy Travis, Senator Slick, and Zsa Zsa, the pig. By the way, how may other writers do you know that have a brother named Olive?

This is an interesting query. The author has written it in a friendly story-like manner, revealing the style of writing that will be found in his manuscript. After reading this letter the editor can make a good judgment about the book's content and the author's skill and wit.

If you are writing fiction, briefly describe the storyline and characters and include the conflict. Keep it short. See the example below.

> My recently completed novel, *Claws*, is a 60,000-word mystery-adventure set in India in 1955. The hero, Arthur Engles, is an explorer hired by an English noble to help find his missing son and to unravel the mystery surrounding his strange disappearance.
>
> Sir Andrew Wellington's son, William, left for an expedition to climb Mt. Everest but was hijacked to India. His traveling companion was found mauled to death by an enormous and apparently supernatural wolf-like creature. Engles and his colleague Harold Smythe, along with Sir Wellington, travel to India and encounter mysterious Russian traders with dubious motives, villagers who may not be what they seem, an unwelcome stranger, and eventually the notorious wolf-creature himself. Suspense is sustained throughout the story by the tension between possible natural and supernatural explanations for the strange events.

For a novel you should keep your description very brief, for you will also include a synopsis or outline which will give the editor a more complete description of your story.

Qualifications

Mention any special training or experience that qualifies you to write the article or book. If the manuscript is on health and fitness, let her know you have a college degree in health, physical therapy, or whatever, and describe the experience you have had in the field. If your article is on prospecting for gold, your qualifications might be the number of years of experience you've had, important discoveries you've made, or successful new techniques you've developed that have brought you recognition from colleagues. You may also mention special awards that acknowledge your achievements.

The following is an example for a finance or business-related topic:

> Over the past 17 years I have created, developed, and sold five successful companies. Currently I am the president of Amalgamated Business Ventures, a business consulting firm. For the last three years I have conducted seminars for the Los Angeles Chamber of Commerce on developing successful businesses.

Example for a manuscript involving guitar music:

> I am a graduate of the Balfor Conservatory of Music. I have been teaching guitar, banjo, and mandolin at Hallmark Music Studio for nine years. I have written and sold over 56 songs, 12 of which have been recorded by famous artists such as Amy Grant, K. T. Oslin, Sandy Patti, and The Judds.

For a book on how to sell real estate:

> I have been a real estate agent for six years. For the past four years, I have been recognized by my company as "Salesman of the Year." Earlier this year I was given the prestigious "Realtor of Excellence" award by the National Realtor's Association.

Writing Experience

If any of your writing has been published, mention that fact and tell who published it. It doesn't have to be a bestselling book or even be published by a large company. It could be a nonpaying publication; it doesn't matter how much you were paid, or if you were even paid at all.

If you are, or have been, a staff writer for a publication, you should mention this fact. It may also be included as part of your qualifications if it relates to the subject you are writing about.

You may mention that you were a winner or finalist in a noted literary contest. But don't bother to tell the editor you won a writing contest in high school or successfully completed a writer's workshop or conference; this type of information means very little to the editor.

If you have been published and are submitting a piece of writing outside the area of your experience, you can simply mention your publishing credits. Don't spend time listing all the publications. If you are writing a western, for example, don't bother to go into length about the poems you've had published. Poetry is a different kind of writing and requires different skills. The same holds true if you write nonfiction and are attempting fiction, or if you write science fiction and are attempting a romance. The writing styles differ for each genre. Just because you have had a cookbook published does not mean you will be a good romance writer.

If you do not have any writing experience, don't call attention to the fact. Let the editor assume, based on your professional presentation, that you are an experienced writer. Don't mention projects you are, or have been, working on if they have not been published. Saying you have written five unpublished novels, says that you like to write but have not demonstrated the skills to get published.

Be honest. I've had authors claim to have had dozens of articles or books published, yet their writing style appears amateurish. Their work is automatically rejected without further consideration. It would have been far better for them to be completely honest and not mention writing credits at all.

The following is an example of how you can mention writing credits:

> I have had three business books published: *How to Buy and Sell a Business*, published by Citadel

> Press, and *Direct Marketing Secrets* and *The Entrepreneur's Business Book,* both published by Houghton Mifflin.

Keep your list of qualifications and writing credits to one or two paragraphs. If they take up more space, put them on a separate sheet of paper. This is usually called an author bio—short for biography. Here you can explain in detail your work and professional experience which qualify you to write the article. List your published writing, who published it, and when. Include any relevant accomplishments or awards. The bio should be written in the third person, as if someone else was talking about you. This is not a resume. Do not mention personal data that has no direct connection to the material you are submitting.

Photographs

Novels and other adult fiction pieces do not normally need photographs. If you are writing a nonfiction book or article, photographs are important. Illustrations will enhance your material and make it more saleable.

If you have photographs available to accompany your manuscript, let the editor know. Having your own photographs will make your manuscript more appealing to the editor, since he won't have to acquire illustrations himself.

Here is an example showing how you can indicate the availability of photos for a book or article on equipment used in certain businesses:

> I have available several quality photographs showing the equipment used in the businesses described in my manuscript.

Normally you will not send your photos with a query letter, but just mention that they are available. You can send copies of the prints if the editor requests to see the manuscript. Photographs are discussed more fully in Chapter 8.

Promotional and Marketing Aids

If you have written a book, let the editor know of ways you can promote and publicize it. Tell him if you have been invited to be interviewed on TV or radio, if you are invited to be a guest speaker, or how your book or article ties in with some current national publicity or event that will help promote the book. If you have promotional or publicity tie-ins with your book, be sure to include this important information in your letter.

Show what publicity the topic has already generated and what is planned or scheduled for the future. Mention special television programs, new movies, or campaigns (political or otherwise), which will advertise your topic. Include important projects sponsored by government, private business, and associations that tie into your subject. Mention anything that will help make the public aware of you or your topic and generate interest in your book. As an example, if the book is related to an Olympic sport, tie it into the Olympics and plan the book so that it can be published in the same year. This way the book can benefit from all of the publicity and public enthusiasm generated by the event.

Publicity generated from various sources is a big plus, publicity the publisher does not have to generate or spend money on. The publisher can ride the tide of current events and capitalize on it, thus making more sales with less expenditures. A presumably ho hum topic will take on new life if you can convince the editor it will have free publicity.

Below is an example for a biography and how the book's subject is receiving publicity.

> The national spotlight has been shining on Debbie Hemner like never before. Debbie's gripping story was revealed to millions of TV viewers last Spring on "Entertainment Tonight." She has recently been featured on NBC's "Today Show," "CBS This Morning," "Cable News Network," "Hard Copy," "Inside Report," and was the subject of a lengthy special feature in

> *Reader's Digest* (March issue "The Incredible Story of Debbie Hemner"). She has also been the focus of high-profile stories in *Woman's World, USA Today, Los Angeles Times, New York Post* and dozens of other magazines and major newspapers throughout the nation. She has plugged my upcoming book on NBC's "Today Show" and in the *New York Post.*

After reading the above paragraph, any editor interested in publishing biographies would take notice. This kind of publicity could definitely generate substantial sales for the book. If you can show that others have an interest in your book's subject and that publicity has been, or is being generated, the sales potential of the book will be greatly enhanced. Here are some additional examples:

> I will appear with Hillary Clinton in November as the recipient of this year's "Woman of the Year" award. I am also scheduled to be a guest on an upcoming segment of "Cincinnati Today," a local TV talk show.

> In February I will be a recipient of the prestigious Norman Vincent Peale "Positive Thinking" award. This award will be presented in Washington D.C. In attendance will be many government figures, including the Vice-President and the Secretary of State. Media coverage will be extensive. There will also be follow-up articles in *Guideposts Magazine* and the *Christian Science Monitor.*

Here is another example:

> This fall I will be starring in a new children's TV program called "Captain Jack's Playhouse." The program will be aired in the Chicago area, which has over six million viewers.

Even though the program will only be shown locally, the number of viewers is substantial. If Captain Jack becomes a celebrity, potential for his book will greatly increase.

An example of the publicity generated by a public speaker is described below:

> I have been teaching this subject in seminars throughout the United States and Canada for five years. I average 40 seminars per year with as many as 300 people registering in each session. I have been featured in *Business Weekly* as well as numerous local newspapers.

This person is publicizing his seminars and teaching thousands of people each year. In this process he is making his name known. Many of those who have attended or contemplated attending his lectures will very likely buy his book.

The next example provides the publisher with information about a new market he might have been unaware of and which might significantly enhance the book's sales.

> My authorized biography of Willard Marriott has been approved by the Marriott Corporation. They have given me a preliminary commitment to buy a minimum of 35 books for each of the gift shops in their 300 hotels in North America. If demand for the books is strong, additional copies will be purchased.

Tie your subject into national and world events. If you write on a subject that is frequently mentioned in the news, you have an audience primed and ready for your material. The downfall of communism in Eastern Europe and the Soviet Union drew tremendous media attention and, consequently, myriads of books and articles. People wanted to know not only about the fall of communism, but about the people, country, and cultures involved. Likewise, the AIDS epidemic, the abortion controversy, and other issues frequently profiled in the media generate public interest. During and after the Persian Gulf War, a slew of books and articles dealing with the military and the Middle East flooded the market. If you can tie your book or article into a current event, your chances of making a sale are greatly improved. This holds true for fiction and nonfiction books or articles.

World shaking news produces much publicity, and a book written and published in a timely manner could benefit greatly from this publicity. However, you don't need a shocking global event to occur before you write. You can tie your material into less dramatic events and still benefit from the publicity. Anniversaries of important historical events always draw attention. The bicentennial of the United States in 1976 was a great time for material dealing with the American Revolution. December 7, 1991 was the anniversary of the Japanese attack on Pearl Harbor and an excellent time to introduce material on that subject. The 500 year anniversary of Columbus' voyage to America has generated public interest and much literature.

Another way of generating interest, commonly used with books, is to show that your material has been endorsed or approved by an association, a celebrity, an authority on the subject, or another respected individual. A foreword by Bob Hope would do wonders for a humor book. His name is recognized and customers would be attracted to the book just for that reason. Even if Hope didn't write a foreword, but just a brief endorsement or review, it would be extremely valuable. Editors love big name endorsements. You may not be able to get an endorsement from a popular celebrity, but you can try to get one from recognized experts on the subject, association officers, and others who will review your manuscript. Reviews and endorsements from neutral sources verify the value of the material. These endorsements can also be used by the publisher to promote your book.

Below is an example of what might be said about endorsements received for the biography of a Hollywood film director:

> My manuscript has received letters of approval from the Directors Guild of America, the American Film Institute Center for Advanced Film Studies, and two educational institutions. Copies are enclosed for your reference.

Your list of endorsements should not extend to telling the editor about all your friends and teachers who have read your work and loved it. Such information is worthless. Editors want quotable reviews and statements from recognized authorities and professionals.

Potential Market

Let the editor know who the book's audience will be. In many cases it is obvious—like for car repair manuals, or gardening books. If you've written a nonfiction book aimed at a particular market—one not now being served—then describe the market, the need, and the reason your book is needed and will be accepted by that market.

Suppose your book was about how to increase computer owners' graphic design and illustration capabilities. Show a need and a market for your book. You might cite an influential source: "*Computer World* magazine states that there are over two million people in the country with computer graphic systems and estimates that 80 percent do not know how to use their equipment to produce effective illustrations." This statement shows the need and potential market. It also shows you've done some research. The editor will take notice.

Let's take another example. If your book is on doll collecting, you may state that there are over 500,000 doll collectors in this country, all of whom are potential customers. There are also four doll related magazines and a doll collectors association. Information like this helps convince the editor that there may be a market for your book and also suggests publicity and marketing angles (reviews, articles, advertisements, available mailing lists) that the publisher could pursue. However, a publisher who specializes in doll books or who has already published books on this subject should already be well aware of these sources and need not be reminded.

Competition

Some publishers will reject a very good book idea simply because they already have a book on the subject or similar books are already available from other publishers. You need to choose a new subject or give a unique slant to a popular topic.

One problem with popular trends or current events is that the subject may quickly become overworked—too many people writing on the same thing. At first, when the topic is new and interest is still growing, almost any well-written piece of material can be published. By the time public interest begins to peak, the subject has probably been covered umpteen times and editors become much more choosy. In order to get your material published, you will need to give it a unique twist or slant, different from all the books already in print. Of course, this advice is true for any material you write; it has got to have a new viewpoint or focus.

Tell the editor what makes your book or article different from all of the others. Research the competition. If you have a book idea, find out what other books have been published on the subject. Show the editor you have done this research by listing the books and explaining why yours is unique. You can find this information in your local library. Look in a directory called *Books in Print*, which lists virtually every book published in the United States and Canada. Also look in the card catalog to see if there are books on the subject that may have gone out of print. You may want to check another directory called *Books Out of Print*. If your book idea is too much like one that has gone out of print, the publisher may not be too enthused.

Closing

In the closing of your letter, make a direct request to the editor for permission to send your proposal or manuscript. The request is important because you are asking the editor to take action and give you a favorable response. This is a positive motivating technique used in advertising. Don't end your letter by just saying "Thank you for your time..." or "The completed manuscript is available if you would care to see it..." or "If you are interested please let me know..." or some similar closing. Be positive. A better ending would be "I look forward to your response." This ending indicates that you expect a response and the editor will feel more obligated to give you one.

If the manuscript is not yet completed, you may specify the completion date and approximate length. Also indicate if you are sending query letters to other publishers. Some publishers refuse to consider multiple submissions, so check with *Writer's Market* before sending your query.

Example for a book-length manuscript:

> Enclosed you will find a synopsis and sample chapters. May I send the complete manuscript to you? This is a simultaneous submission. I'm looking forward to your response.

Example for an article:

> I can have the 2,000-word article completed by July 1. Would you be interested? This is an exclusive query. I look forward to hearing from you soon.

The Completed Letter

You now know all of the elements that need to be included in a good query letter. I recommend that you write several query letters for practice. Your skill at creating good query letters will improve as you gain experience writing them. If you have a writing project finished or in progress, use that topic as your subject.

On the following page is an example of a completed query letter for a magazine article:

> What questions will an employer ask in a job interview? What questions should you ask in an interview? What kind of clothes are an instant turnoff to prospective employers? How do you convince an employer that you are the best person for the job? These are just some of the questions that will be answered by my proposed article "Super Job Interviews."
>
> I am in the process of surveying resource executives in 50 of the top Fortune 500 companies to find out what job candidates need to say and do to get the right job in today's tough job market. The article will explain how to make a positive impression, what to say and what not to say, how to present your qualifications to suit an employer's needs, what you should know about a company, and how to prepare yourself before an interview. Readers will learn what employers are looking for in job applicants and how to avoid common mistakes.
>
> I have had twelve years experience working with employers and job applicants. Currently, I am president of The Employment Connection, a human resources consulting firm specializing in career transition counseling for displaced employees. I have previously had articles published in *Money Magazine,* and *Income Opportunities.*
>
> I can have this 3,500-word article finished by April 30. May I write the article for you? Thank you for considering my proposal. I await your reply.

Enclose a self-addressed stamped return envelope. Use a #10 business-sized envelope. The editor will use this to send you a reply. If you don't include a return envelope, you will hear from the editor only if he is interested in seeing your work. If not, he will simply trash your letter without sending a response.

It is important for you to be persistent and not to get discouraged or give up after receiving several rejections. It is not unusual for an author to receive 10-20 rejections before finding the right publisher. Some authors have received many more rejections than this before selling their work and, eventually, ending up with a bestseller or winning a Pulitzer Prize. This shows that even some of the best manuscripts can be hard to sell. So don't give up too easily.

REJECTION PROOF YOUR QUERY

A key to making a good impression on an editor is to present yourself in a professional manner. In this chapter you have learned what your query letter should look like and what it should contain. By following these guidelines you will give the editor the impression that you are a professional. Whether you are already published or not, your material *will* receive more careful consideration than it would otherwise.

If you follow all of the advice in this chapter, you can still tip off the editor that you are an unpublished amateur by making some inadvertent comments. Although editors will look at any well-written query with an open mind, they all have a subconscious resistance to unpublished authors. A few careless statements can give you away, especially in that most revealing opening paragraph.

I believe that you can learn a lot from the mistakes of others. Therefore, I have included a few examples of ineffective opening statements in query letters. These comments are from actual letters I have received. Ask yourself what's wrong with them.

> I am not a salesman and have no idea of how to write an award winning query letter that will entice you to read my manuscript. I do have, what I believe, is a funny novel that deserves to be read.

> Enclosed please find a few short stories I recently came up with. I have several more, but why waste

> postage if you don't like the style? I have never done this before and I'm not sure if I'm going about this correctly.
>
> I apologize for the form letter but my printer is acting up. It probably wouldn't make it through a number of near letter quality letters.
>
> An informal survey reveals that 86.3% of the people in the United States believe they have the talent to be a professional writer. I am one of them. Accordingly, over the years I have written a story here and some lines of verse there and have assembled them into a book.
>
> I enclose a manuscript, "Travis Coefood, Unknown Celebrity, which I hereby submit for your consideration. I am author of more than 50 published articles and three published books.

I could give many more examples, but these will suffice. What's wrong with these opening statements? Plenty, but the biggest fault is that they lack professionalism. They contain grammar errors, offer useless information, advertise the fact they are amateurs, and project a sloppy attitude, which indicate that work from these authors will probably be poorly written and unpublishable. How can a publisher take them seriously if they are not willing to take the time to properly prepare submission materials?Publishing is a business and editors want to do business with other professionals.

Query Letter Don'ts

Novice writers frequently make comments that reveal their publishing ignorance and lack of preparation. Take heed of the following list of query letter don'ts:

- Don't tell the editor you're an unpublished author.

- Don't advise the editor about the cover art, book size and shape, page layout, or price. Most authors have no comprehension of the factors that influence the publisher's decisions on these matters. This is his area of expertise; let him make the decisions.

- Don't make references to money, advances, or royalties. Let the editor approach you on these subjects.

- Don't try to be cute or funny. You are writing a business letter and should conduct yourself in a professional manner.

- Don't say anything that is not absolutely necessary. The longer the letter is, the less likely it is to be read.

- Don't ask for advice or suggestions. Only a novice would send in a submission which he or she felt was so imperfect it needed additional editorial feedback.

- Don't claim to have written the next bestseller. Predicting the success of a book is extremely difficult, even for seasoned editors. If editors could always tell which books were going to be bestsellers, they wouldn't be publishing so many that weren't.

- Don't tell the editor "I have written a humorous book..." If it's funny, your book will prove the point.

- Don't be redundant. "I have written a fictional novel..."

- Don't make false statements about your experience or publishing credits. Your writing skills will be plainly evident in your submission. Give names and dates of writing credits. If your list of credits is long, add an author biography.

- Don't tell the editor that your friends loved the book. All aspiring authors' friends tell them that.

- Don't misspell the editor's name. Some editors feel that this is a sign of carelessness that will also be reflected in the author's writing.

- Don't forget to carefully proofread your letter and correct all spelling, grammatical, punctuation, and typographical errors.

For more information about writing query letters I would recommend reading *How to Write Irresistible Query Letters* by Lisa Collier Cool.

CHAPTER 7

BOOK PROPOSALS

A query letter or book proposal will be the first thing you will send to a book publisher to interest him in your manuscript. Do not send the complete manuscript unless it is requested. Unsolicited manuscripts are often rejected unread, or given little consideration. Sending a query letter or book proposal first will keep your manuscript out of the slush pile and place it in the hands of an interested editor.

Some book publishers prefer to receive a query letter before being sent a book proposal. These publishers may respond to a query letter by requesting either a book proposal or the entire manuscript. Most publishers, however, will accept book proposals with the initial query. Published writers often use proposals to sell their books before the manuscripts are even completed. A decision to buy and publish your manuscript may be made solely on the merits of your proposal. If you want to sell your book, you will need to prepare a professional looking book proposal.

There is no one correct way to prepare a book proposal. It can be as short or as long as you feel is necessary to adaquately describe your book. What is importent is that you include enough information so that the editor can make an accurate judgment of your project.

Most book proposals are composed of some combination of a cover letter, an introduction, a synopsis, an outline, and sample chapters. The exact combination of these will depend on the type of book you have and what the publisher wants, as indicated in *Writer's Market.*

COVER LETTER

You will always include a cover letter with your book proposal. If your book proposal is your *initial* contact with the publisher, the cover letter acts as a query letter and should contain the same information as a query letter.

If, however, you sent the publisher a query letter first and he requested a proposal, the cover letter should not be a repeat of your query letter or used to make another sales pitch. Keep it to a paragraph or two and briefly remind the editor that he requested the material. (See the example on the following page.)

Since it is the story that sells fiction, if you have written a novel, your initial contact with the publisher should be a proposal. In that case your cover letter functions as a query letter.

For nonfiction books it is best to send a query letter first. An editor is much more willing to read a one or two-page letter than he is a 50-page proposal. Also, he has a much easier decision to make. You are not asking him to make a purchase, you are merely asking him to take a look at your proposal. If he responds positively to your letter, he will be prepared for it when it comes; it will not be an unsolicited submission. And since he requested it, he now owes you a personal response. *This requires that he actually read your material.* This way your submission will get into the hands of the right person and be given a fair evaluation. If, however, you send the book proposal first, you might only get a form rejection letter and you will never really know if anyone actually looked at your material.

Audrey Hamilton
4417 Butler Avenue
Denver, CO 80944
(303) 574-8393

March 15, 19—

Mary Roe
Submissions Editor
Amalgamated Publications
101 Broadway
New York, NY 10011

Dear Ms. Roe:

Thank you for your response to my query letter regarding my book *Guide to Self-Publishing*. Enclosed you will find a detailed outline and samples of the first three chapters.

I look forward to your response and for the opportunity to submit the entire manuscript for your examination.

Yours truly,

Audrey Hamilton

Enclosures: outline, sample chapters

An example of a cover letter accompanying a requested book proposal.

This is another important key or trick of the trade you should remember in order to avoid having your manuscript needlessly rejected.

When writing your query or cover letter, follow the suggestions outlined in the previous chapter about query letters.

An example of a query letter that would accompany a book proposal:

> I have written a 60,000-word manuscript, entitled *How to Write Great Ads,* which teaches the skill of writing effective advertising for print ads, direct mail packages, and radio and television commercials.
>
> This book demystifies the process of writing advertising, using a step-by-step process and workbook format. It breaks down the ad writing process into a series of simple steps. Included are fill-in exercises and other self-tests for practicing each step immediately after learning it. This book helps would-be ad writers to quickly learn to write effective ad pieces, and feel confident.
>
> Enclosed you will find a chapter-by-chapter outline of the book and three sample chapters.
>
> There are only three other books currently in print on ad copywriting—all of which were written over nine years ago and are essentially outdated. My book incorporates the newest trends and developments in this field, including the latest statistics and marketing studies.
>
> I have a degree in communications from Harvard University. For the past fifteen years I have worked as an advertising copywriter and presently am vice-president of Classic Advertising Agency in Los Angeles. I have been teaching copywriting for the University of Southern California Continuing Education Department for six years. I was the recipient of the 1993 California Copywriter's Association's "Copywriter of the Year" award.
>
> My manuscript has been endorsed by the Dean of the School of Business at USC. As a part-time

> instructor at that institution, I will use this book as a required text and recommend it to other professors at USC and elsewhere. As the newly elected Education Director of the California Copywriter's Association, I will strongly promote and publicize the book among my colleagues.
>
> May I send you a copy of *How to Write Great Ads?* This is a simultaneous submission. I look forward to your reply.

This query letter is direct and to the point. It doesn't waste the editor's time or try his patience with a hard driving sales talk expounding all the merits of the book.

INTRODUCTION TO THE PROPOSAL

Some nonfiction book proposals may include an introduction which would contain much of the same information mentioned in the query letter, but in more detail. You would use an introduction if this information cannot be adaquately covered in a two-page query letter. Novels don't need an introduction because everything the editor needs to know about the book can be stated in a short cover letter.

The introduction consists of an overview of the project describing the scope and content of the book, including information on promotion, marketing, and competition. If you have extensive professional qualifications or writing credits, that information would also be included in the introduction on a separate sheet of paper under the heading "About the Author."

If you include an introduction to your proposal, you can reduce your cover letter to simply the opening and closing statements as described in the last chapter. You may also add a title page. Do not staple or bind your proposal. Label each page with your name, an abreviated book title, and page number. See the examples on page 95.

SYNOPSIS

Publishers will usually request either a synopsis or an outline as part of your proposal. They both serve a similar purpose. Often, the terms are used interchangeably and what you send to the publisher will depend on the type of manuscript you have and whether or not it is complete. Basically, a synopsis is a brief description of your book, while an outline is longer and more detailed. Both the synopsis and the outline should be typed in manuscript form as described in Chapter 8.

A synopsis is primarily used when you have a completed manuscript available and ready to send to the editor. It is a brief descriptive summary of your book, limited to just a few pages. Its purpose is to interest the editor in your manuscript so that he will request to see it (thus avoiding the unsolicited manuscript barrier).

Make it interesting and easy to read. The synopsis not only describes your book, but also gives the editor a sample of your writing style and ability. If your synopsis does not flow smoothly or contains spelling, grammar, and punctuation errors, the editor knows the manuscript will be the same, and he won't be interested. Reread and rewrite your synopsis as many times as necessary until it is as good as you can possibly make it. Don't kill your chance of submitting your manuscript with a hastily written synopsis.

OUTLINE

While the purpose of the synopsis is to convince the editor to read your manuscript, the purpose of the outline is to convince the editor to *buy* your manuscript. The editor may buy your idea and commission you to complete the manuscript, or he may request to see the completed manuscript before he makes an offer. Whether or not your manuscript is complete, you can send an outline.

Parts to a nonfiction book proposal.

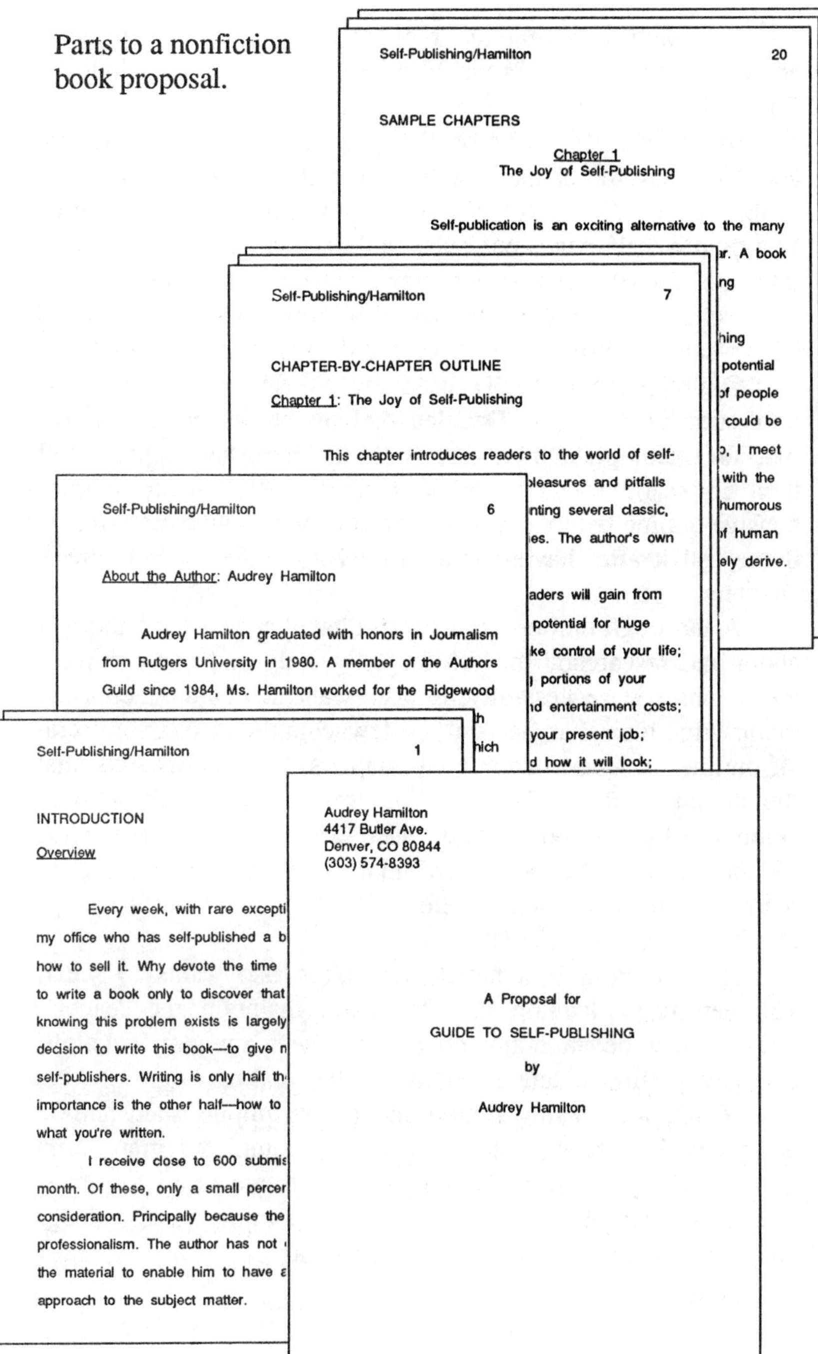

Self-Publishing/Hamilton 20

SAMPLE CHAPTERS

Chapter 1
The Joy of Self-Publishing

Self-publication is an exciting alternative to the many
...r. A book
...ng
...hing
... potential
...of people
... could be
...o, I meet
... with the
... humorous
...of human
...ely derive.

Self-Publishing/Hamilton 7

CHAPTER-BY-CHAPTER OUTLINE

Chapter 1: The Joy of Self-Publishing

This chapter introduces readers to the world of self-
...pleasures and pitfalls
...nting several classic,
...ies. The author's own
...aders will gain from
... potential for huge
...ke control of your life;
... portions of your
...nd entertainment costs;
... your present job;
...d how it will look;

Self-Publishing/Hamilton 6

About the Author: Audrey Hamilton

Audrey Hamilton graduated with honors in Journalism from Rutgers University in 1980. A member of the Authors Guild since 1984, Ms. Hamilton worked for the Ridgewood
...h
...hich

Self-Publishing/Hamilton 1

INTRODUCTION

Overview

Every week, with rare excepti...
my office who has self-published a b...
how to sell it. Why devote the time ...
to write a book only to discover that...
knowing this problem exists is largely...
decision to write this book—to give n...
self-publishers. Writing is only half th...
importance is the other half—how to ...
what you're written.

I receive close to 600 submis...
month. Of these, only a small percen...
consideration. Principally because the...
professionalism. The author has not ...
the material to enable him to have a...
approach to the subject matter.

Audrey Hamilton
4417 Butler Ave.
Denver, CO 80844
(303) 574-8393

A Proposal for

GUIDE TO SELF-PUBLISHING

by

Audrey Hamilton

The outline covers the plot or highlights of your book chapter by chapter and is much more detailed than the synopsis. The outline of each chapter may run from one paragraph to two or more pages, depending on the type of book you are writing and how long the chapters will be. For most books a page per chapter is usually plenty. If your outline for each chapter runs less than a half page, put each outline one after the other. If they are longer, put each chapter on a separate page. Outline every chapter including the ones you send as samples so the editor can see how each chapter progresses to the next.

Outlines are normally used for novels and uncompleted nonfiction manuscripts. Detailed outlines are especially important for incomplete manuscripts. Most published authors sell their books by way of a book proposal containing a comprehensive outline before they have finished writing the manuscript. Some sell it after having written only a couple of preliminary chapters.

A thorough outline shows the editor that you have thought about and researched the subject adequately and can complete the manuscript successfully. Editors want to avoid accepting a manuscript idea that has only a few completed chapters with an outline of several additional chapters, only to discover that the author couldn't find much more to say—resulting in a skimpy, 84-page book. Editors also wish to avoid having the second half of the book turn into a philosophical platform inappropriate to the rest of the book. A detailed outline helps eliminate these problems.

If your work is a novel, the editor also wants to see if you can fully develop the story and maintain the reader's interest. Include all major characters, the main plot, subplots, and any pertinent details, including the ending.

If you are writing fiction and are an unpublished author, editors will probably want to see your completed manuscript before making an offer. Nonfiction writers are more fortunate. The value of a nonfiction book is derived from the knowledge and information it contains rather than its ability to entertain.

Even a first-time author can sell an uncompleted nonfiction manuscript from a well-written book proposal.

The completed manuscript does not have to follow your proposed outline exactly. Editors realize that as you write the book, new ideas will emerge, or concepts may need to be separated or combined. Often, editor's suggestions will lead to changes.

Although you will not include dialogue or be too descriptive or flowery in the outline, you should make the material as interesting as possible. Editors don't want to read something dry and boring, especially for a novel. Avoid using the passive voice. Focus on the action, characters, and plot.

Often, particularly with medium and large publishing houses, an in-house editor must convince superiors to buy the book. A well-written outline will help. The senior editors, who will probably never read the book, will make the decisions based, in part, on the junior editor's enthusiasm and the outline.

On pages 98-99 are examples showing how to set up your outline. Although different formats can be used, the example shown here is acceptable to most publishers. If a publisher wants the proposal or outline formatted in a certain way, he will indicate this in his author's guidelines. Guidelines are free for the asking if you send a self-addressed stamped business envelope.

SAMPLE CHAPTERS

Most publishers prefer to see sample chapters before requesting the entire manuscript. You should send two to three chapters unless specified otherwise in *Writer's Market*. Some publishers will indicate they want certain chapters, while others will leave that decision up to the author or agent. The publisher may require the first three chapters so that he can see how the author develops the book. Another may want the first, a middle, and the last chapter to see how it begins, progresses, and ends. Most

Self-Publishing/Hamilton 7

CHAPTER-BY-CHAPTER OUTLINE

Chapter 1: The Joy of Self-Publishing

This chapter introduces readers to the world of self-publishing by describing some of the pleasures and pitfalls self-publishers face. It begins by recounting several classic, as well as contemporary, success stories. The author's own success story is highlighted.

An overview of the rewards readers will gain from self-publishing includes: discussing the potential for huge financial profits; getting a chance to take control of your life; tax shelter benefits, including deducting portions of your home, as well as automobile, travel, and entertainment costs; beginning this business while keeping your present job; having total control over your book and how it will look; publishing your book much more quickly than a trade publisher; and finally, the exciting and satisfying experience of seeing your book completed and in print.

The drawbacks include the responsibility of performing or supervising the many different functions involved in self-publishing: writing, editing, design, typesetting, printing, accounting, finance, shipping, promotion, and business management. Another serious consideration is the high cost of preparing, producing, and marketing a book. You must also be willing to

The first page of the chapter-by-chapter outline for the *Guide to Self-Publishing*.

Self-Publishing/Hamilton 8

devote a considerable amount of time and energy to making your book successful.

The chapter will conclude with a summary of the advantages versus the disadvantages of self-publishing and the reasons why many people feel the positive aspects outweigh the drawbacks.

The second page of the outline for the *Guide to Self-Publishing*.

publishers let you choose the chapters to send. The material should total between 30 to 60 pages. You need to send a sample long enough to demonstrate your writing skill.

If I receive sample chapters other than the first three, I know that the author has given me the three best chapters he has. Those three chapters had better be something special because I suspect the rest of the book might not be as good. However, if an author sends me the first three chapters, I consider them to be representative of the entire manuscript and will not be so critical. Unless specified otherwise, you should always send the first three chapters. If they are not the most interesting in your manuscript, then maybe you need to revise your manuscript. The first chapter, particularly, should be interesting enough to entice potential readers to continue reading.

With the information I have provided in this chapter, you can now prepare a book proposal that will meet the expectations of editors. For a more detailed discussion on writing and preparing proposals I recommend reading the book *How to Write a Book Proposal* by Michael Larsen.

CHAPTER 8

MANUSCRIPT PREPARATION

As a publisher, I receive scores of manuscripts every year. They come to me in an assortment of styles and formats. Some follow the guidelines for proper manuscript preparation, many do not. Either consciously or subconsciously the appearance of each manuscript affects my attitude toward it.

Editors judge a work by the way it looks even before they read it. Some editors will reject a manuscript without reading it simply because it is messy or was not typed in an acceptable format. You should never let your manuscript be rejected for this reason. It is a very simple matter to type and present a manuscript properly.

Although the appearance and structure of a manuscript says a lot about the author, slight variations in the format are perfectly acceptable. There is no one correct way to prepare a manuscript. A publisher will not reject a manuscript simply because you inserted an extra space below the title. Publishers are not that picky. Professional writers use somewhat different formats, but their manuscripts all follow generally accepted guidelines and are easy to read. I will describe how to properly prepare your manuscript in a neat and professional-looking format. I recommend that you follow the format I describe as closely as possible. Too much deviation will only make you look like an amateur and reduce your chances of getting published.

A manuscript that doesn't follow the accepted format signals to the editor that the writer is an amateur, lacks knowledge of the publishing and writing profession, and is too lazy to learn the proper submission procedures. This suggests the writing in the manuscript will be second-rate.

If you can present your work in a professional manner, I guarantee your manuscript will pass the first round of rejections and will be given careful consideration from editors.

CREATING A PROFESSIONAL APPEARANCE

Editors' time is precious. They like material that is easy to read. For this reason, handwritten manuscripts are totally unacceptable. Dot-matrix computer printouts are usually undesirable and many editors won't accept them unless they are near letter-quality. Use a good typewriter or printer that can produce letter-quality characters. Laser printers do an excellent job, and although not necessary, they do give a good impression.

Avoid using old, worn-out typewriters or ribbons that blur the letters, fill ink in the loops (e.g., d, e), or can't type in a consistently straight line. Get the typewriter fixed, buy a new one, or have someone type the manuscript for you, but make it neat. Do not cross out or put XXs through typographical errors, and avoid making corrections by hand with a pen. A few errors can be corrected with correction tape or fluids. If there are too many errors, retype the page!

A great manuscript will go unread if the type style is not easy to read. Don't use all capital letters, cursive, or any other fancy type style. With computers and laser printers, there is a temptation to use fancy fonts, but don't. The easier the manuscript is to read, the better your chances of getting it read. Use a standard type style for all of your submission materials.

Use good quality, 20-pound bond, 8½ x 11-inch, white paper for your manuscript. Type on only one side of the sheet. All the margins on the page should be at least 1 to 1¼ inches. Do not staple the sheets together. You may use a paper clip to hold them together if you desire.

If you print from a computer on fanfold paper with tractor edges, strip off the feeder strips and separate the pages before you send them. Make sure the characters are clear and dark enough to be easily read.

Some publishers will accept electronic submissions (over a modem or on disk). However, do not send a submission over a modem or fax unless you are specifically invited to do so by the editor.

MANUSCRIPT COVER LETTERS

If you are submitting your manuscript to a publisher who will consider a complete manuscript on the initial contact, your cover letter should give the editor a brief description of the book and tell him something about yourself, your qualifications, and publishing history, just like the query letter. You usually do not need to include a synopsis or an outline.

A cover letter should always accompany your manuscript. If an editor receives a manuscript with no cover letter she may not know what type of book it is or for what audience it is written. Rather than spend time trying to figure this out, she may simply decide not to read your manuscript, or put it aside until later, giving preference to other submissions. Busy editors at large publishing companies would automatically reject it.

Most manuscripts are (or should be) sent to publishers after receiving a positive response to a query letter or book proposal. If the manuscript was sent on request from the editor, the cover letter acts only as a reminder that he requested it. You have already sent your query letter and don't need to restate that information. Don't make another sales pitch; let the manuscript speak for itself.

MANUSCRIPT FORMAT

Title Page

Use a title page for book-length manuscripts. If you are submitting an article or short story, a title page is not necessary.

Whether you use a title page or not, the first page of the manuscript will contain important information about you and your work. This information is put at the top of the first page of the manuscript and should be single-spaced.

In the upper left hand corner, type your name (use your real name, not a pseudonym), mailing address, and daytime phone number.

In the upper right hand corner of the first page, indicate the approximate number of words in the manuscript. This is important because publishers have a word range they must work within. Because of limited space magazine publishers must have an accurate word count. If your article is too long (even by a few sentences), something will be cut. If it is too short, you will be asked to add to it.

If you have written a magazine article, indicate what rights you are offering for sale below the word count. Normally, you offer first serial rights, which means the publication has the right to publish the article for the first time in any periodical. (See Chapter 5 for a more complete discussion of rights.)

You may also put a copyright notice under the rights statement if you wish. This is done by typing the word "copyright" or the symbol "©" followed by the year and your name. A handwritten copyright symbol is acceptable. The copyright notice is optional.

If you are using a title page (book-length manuscripts), do not number it or include it in the total page count. If you do not use a title page (articles), do not number the first page, but do include it in the total page count.

Come one-third of the way down the page and type the title. It should be centered and in all capital letters. Double-space after the title and type "by," double-space again and type your name or pseudonym. The line with your name is referred to as your *byline.*

If you have a book-length manuscript and are using an agent, put the agent's name, address, and phone number on the lower right hand side of the title page. If you do not have an agent, leave the rest of the page blank. Your title page is now complete. Page 106 shows an example of a title page for a book-length manuscript.

If you have an article or short story, you will begin the text below the byline.

The Text

For book-length manuscripts begin each chapter about one-third of the page down from the top. Type the chapter number, double-space, and the chapter title in all capital letters. Drop down two double-spaces and begin the body of your manuscript. See the example on page 107.

For an article, where you are not using a separate title page, drop down two double-spaces below your byline and indent five spaces from the left margin. Now begin the body of your manuscript. The body of the manuscript should be double-spaced. Indent each paragraph five spaces. See page 109 for an example of an article.

Headers and Footers

Since your manuscript is not stapled or permanently bound together, each page must be identified. Put your name and the page number on a single line on every page after the first. This is called the *slug line.* The slug line will keep pages in order and prevent them from getting lost if they are accidently mixed with someone else's material.

The slug line can be placed near any of the four corners of the page. If it is placed at the top of the page, it is called a *header* and if it is placed at the bottom of the page, it is called a *footer.* The most common place for the slug line is at the upper left corner of the page.

Robin Flanders
P.O. Box 1222
New York, NY 10012
(212) 223-4321

96,400 words

ON THE HIGH SEAS

by

Robin Flanders

The title page for a book-length manuscript.

High Seas/Flanders 1

CHAPTER 1
THE ADVENTURE BEGINS

I was born in the year 1632, in the city of York, of a good family. My father earned a good estate by merchandise in London, and leaving off his trade, retired at York; from whence he had married my mother.

I had two elder brothers, one of whom was a lieutenant-colonel but was killed at the battle near Dunkirk against the Spaniards. What became of my second brother I never knew, any more than my father or mother knew what became of me.

Being the third son of the family, and not bred to any trade, my head began to be filled very early with rambling thoughts. My father, who was very ancient, had given me a competent share of learning, as far as house education and a country free school generally goes, and designed me

The first page of a book-length manuscript after the title page. Page numbering starts on this page.

High Seas/Flanders 312

In the meantime, I in part settled myself here. For, first of all, I married, and had three children, two sons and one daughter. But my wife dying, and my nephew coming home, with good success, from a voyage to Spain, my inclination to go abroad, and his importunity, prevailed, and I engaged to go in his ship as a private trader to the East Indies. In this voyage I visited my new colony in the island, saw my successors, and had the whole story of their coming to the island, after my departure. All these things, with some very surprising incidents, in some new adventures of my own, for ten year more, I may, perhaps, give a farther account of hereafter.

The End

The last manuscript page of a novel.

Susan Williams
443 Park Avenue
New York, NY 10011
(212) 543-4433

3,000 words
First Serial Rights

FOOTWEAR FACTS

by

Susan Williams

Man is the "tenderfoot" among animals, so in very ancient times he began to fashion some sort of foot covering for protection from the burning sands and the stony ground. The animals could leave all this to nature, for they were provided either with soft cushions like those on the feet of the cat or with horny hoofs like those of the horse.

Man's earliest footwear was the sandal. Mats of woven grass, strips of hide, or flat pieces of wood to protect the soles of the feet were fastened by thongs over the foot, or sometimes brought up between the toes and bound around the ankle. In time, more material was

The first manuscript page of an article. For an article the page numbering starts on the second page. No separate title page is used.

Footwear/Williams 2

the cold, and the sandal became the shoe. The Greeks and the Romans worked out a variety of decorative sandals, and some of the Romans styles approached the shoe form. In colder regions some of the first shoes were mere bags padded with grass and tied about the feet. Sometimes the skins of animals were made into moccasins or clumsy boots.

Modern footwear had its beginning in the Middle Ages. In the feudal days, the craftsmen who fashioned the footwear for the castle lords and ladies were very important. Substantial footwear was necessary in the cold northern climates, and persons who took part in the Crusades or went on long pilgrimages needed durable shoes. Furthermore, the barons and knights paid a great deal of attention to their appearance, and to please them their craftsmen showed great individuality in working out a variety of slippers, shoes, and boots. Some were made with and some without heels. Some were adorned with great buckles. Fashions ran to ridiculous extremes. In the 13th and 14th centuries it was fashionable to wear long narrow-toed shows; the higher the rank of the wearer, the longer the toes.

The second manuscript page of an article.

Footwear/Williams 12

The shoe is now ready for heeling and this is done on the "lightning heeling machine," so called from the speed with which it works. The heels are built up of different lifts of leather, glued together, and put under pressure to make them durable and shapely. After the heels are attached, a "slugging" machine drives metal pieces of "slugs" into the bottom of the heel, at the places where most of the wear comes. Then machines grind the heel and the surface is smoothed with sandpaper and buffing machines.

The shoes with the soles and heels attached are then sent into the finishing room. There the soles are smoothed and polished; the uppers, sides of the heels, and the edges of the soles are blackened and polished; the trademark of the manufacturer is stamped on the sole—and the shoes are ready for market.

- 30 -

The last manuscript page of an article.

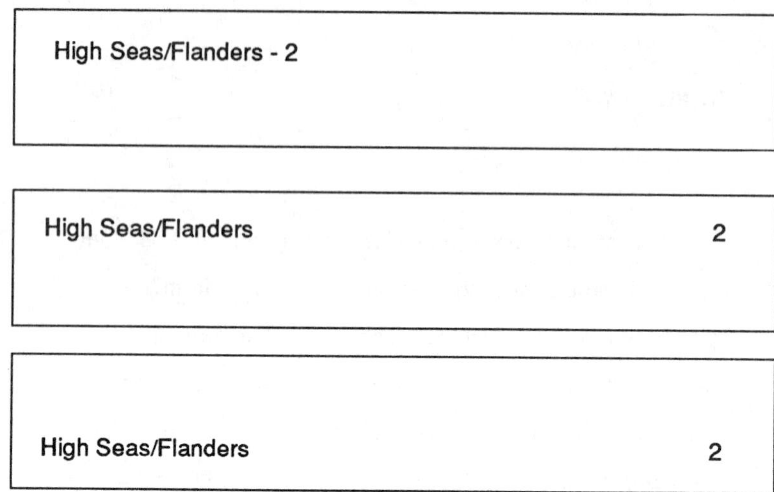

Examples of slug lines.

The slug line can take one of several possible forms. What's important is that essential information is included. Type a shortened form of the title, a slash, your last name, a dash, and then the page number. The page number can come immediately after your name or be positioned toward the far right side of the page. The book title, chapter title, or chapter number can be typed on this line or beneath it, if you desire.

If you are using a pseudonym, type your real name, followed by your pen name in parentheses and the page number. For example, Flanders (Schultz) - 2. Double-space twice and resume typing the text.

If you are writing a book, begin each chapter on a new page and include a slug line with the page number. Follow the examples on pages 107-111.

Front and Back Matter

Front matter and back matter are parts of books, but not part of the main text. Front matter includes the table of contents, dedication, acknowledgements, preface, list of illustrations or tables, and foreword. Back matter includes an appendix, bibliography, glossary, list of abbreviations, and index. Not all of these are needed or contained in every book or manuscript. The index, for example, is almost always compiled after the manuscript has been set up in book form. Novels do not normally need a table of contents, foreword, or list of tables, and the like. A table of contents should, however, be added to nonfiction manuscripts.

You do not normally need to put page numbers on front matter, as they are usually compiled after the rest of the manuscript. But you can put page numbers on the back matter. A slug line with title and author is always included.

All front and back matter is prepared in basically the same manner. The slug line is typed about an inch below the top of the page (if you are using a header). Drop down about a third of a page, center, and type the heading in all capital letters. Drop down two double-spaces and type the text. An example of a foreword is on page 114.

Ending

After the last sentence of the manuscript, if it is a work of fiction, drop down three double-spaces and center the words "The End" to indicate the end of the manuscript. If it is nonfiction, use "###" or the symbol "- 30 -" which signifies the same thing. See the examples on pages 107 and 110.

ESTIMATING WORD COUNT

If you do your writing on a compuer, your program may automatically give you the exact word count. If you don't have this option available, you must approximate this number. Accurate estimation of the total number of words in your manuscript is important to the publisher. This should not be an educated guess, but a very close approximation. A variety of methods can be used to estimate the total number of words. If you have a book-length manuscript, count the exact number

High Seas/Flanders

FOREWORD

No more striking figure can be found in all the dramatic history of France than that of Jean du Plessis, who as admiral of king Louis XIII's navy, controlled for nearly 20 years the destinies of France and raised her to the position of the foremost power in Europe. Haughty, stern, ruthless, implacable, the great admiral is a figure that kindles the imagination and has been the theme of countless paintings, dramas, and romances. Even when sickly and wasted with disease, such was the force of his will and the majesty of his bearing that he over-awed all, including the king. He loved the privileges and trappings of power, living in royal state, and forcing even princes to yield him place. Not even the most powerful noble in the realm dared to stand against him. Every whisper of plot or

An example of a foreword.

of words in three full pages of your manuscript. Do not use the first or the last page or the first page of a chapter. Count all the words, including abbreviations and short words (e.g., a, I, me), as one word each. Divide the number you get by three and multiply that by the total number of pages in the manuscript. Round this number to the nearest 100 words.

If this process is new to you, it may sound a bit confusing. Let's look at an example using a 100-page manuscript. If the total number of words on three pages of your manuscript were 805, you would divide 805 by 3 to get the average number of words on each page, which in this case is 268.33. Multiplying 268.33 by the total number of pages, which is 100, gives you 26,833. Now rounding this number off to the nearest 100 gives you a page count of 26,800 words.

The estimation can be made quicker for article-length manuscripts. Count the number of words in 10 full lines of the manuscript. Divide this number by 10 to find the average words per line. Multiple this number by the number of lines on a page to find the words per page. Multiply the number of words per page by the total number of pages to get your word count.

COPYRIGHTS

The copyright law gives legal protection to the creators of original works of authorship. It is good for the lifetime of the author plus 50 years. This protection is available to both published and unpublished works. Copyright protection begins from the time a work is created and immediately becomes the property of the author. In the case where a work was "made for hire," that is, prepared by an employee within the scope of his or her employment or when the work was specially commissioned for use as a collective work, the employer and not the employee is considered the author. Copyright protection covers only the author's verbal or illustrative presentation of the work. It does not extend to ideas, procedures, concepts, principles, or discoveries.

Although many writers like to include a copyright statement

on their manuscripts, it isn't necessary. Anything you write is automatically copyrighted. You do not need to have it registered with the Copyright Office, have a lawyer verify it, or do anything else. As soon as you write something, it becomes your property. A problem arises only when there is a dispute over who is the legal author of a work. Copyright ownership is proved by establishing who had a documented claim to the work first. This is best done by having the work registered with the Copyright Office. Registration does not give you the copyright, it only verifies that you have claimed ownership. You can put a copyright notice on *anything* you write, but it does not necessarily mean that it has been registered.

Putting a copyright notice on your manuscript actually means nothing. Publishers are quite aware of the copyright law and they know your work is legally yours, so making such a claim is redundant. In fact, stating that your material is copyrighted is somewhat offensive. In essence what the author is saying is that he does not trust the publisher and is warning him not to steal his work.

If you submit your material to a publisher listed in *Writer's Market* or other similar directories, you do not need to worry about them stealing your work. That's the last thing they will do. Why would they risk their reputations and perhaps even the existence of their businesses by doing such a thing? They would more than likely get caught because the author would probably have some proof of ownership. It would be much more beneficial for the publisher to acquire the book under normal procedures because he can then work with the author to boost sales. Having the author participate in publicizing the book (e.g., book signings, talk show appearances, etc.) can increase sales tremendously. So you do not have to worry about a legitimate publisher stealing your work.

You don't even need to get your work registered with the Copyright Office. If a publisher buys your work, he will automatically register it for you, in your name (unless you have sold him these rights). The publisher will fill out the government forms, pay the required fee, and send in copies of the work as required by the Copyright Office. This is done *after* the book has been printed because the Copyright Office requires copies of the completed books. A manuscript can be registered too, but this is generally a waste of time and money because once the book is published, it will have to be registered again.

I have one more comment about putting a copyright notice on your manuscript. Sometimes I'll receive a manuscript with a copyright notice whose date is a year or two old. What does this say? It tells me that the manuscript has been floating around to various publishers for many months or even years without success. My immediate impression is that the manuscript must not be very good or it would have been sold by now and the author is sending it to me as a last resort. (He probably sent it to all the big publishers first.) With these negative thoughts, I am automatically prejudiced against the manuscript before I know anything about it. If the manuscript is even read, I will do it very critically. I am sure other editors react the same way.

So, I believe it is better to leave the copyright notice off the manuscript entirely. It serves no practical purpose and may even hamper the chances of selling your work.

PERMISSIONS

At times you may want to use material from a published source. If you use any illustrations from a publication that is protected by copyright, you must get permission, in writing, from the publisher. The same is true of written material, with certain exceptions.

The copyright law allows the use of some written material without the permission of the copyright owner. Factors which influence this "fair use" of copyrighted material include the nature and purpose of the use, the amount of the work used in relation to the length of the original, and the effect of the use on the commercial value of the work from which the material is taken. There is no strict rule by which to judge what constitutes fair use, which leaves it up to the courts to decide in individual cases where the copyright holder has claimed infringement. For a 500-page novel, several paragraphs could be considered fair use. But for a one-page poem a single sentence could constitute infringement.

If you use material without prior consent, it must not constitute a significant amount of the entire work. Nor can it devalue the original work. For example, if the original work devotes 50 pages towards identifying or making a significant conclusion, you cannot copy this conclusion, even though it may only constitute a small portion of the entire text.

If you want to use more than a few paragraphs from a book or several sentences from an article, you probably should get permission first.

To obtain permission, write a letter to the publisher's permissions department. Identify exactly the material you wish to use. Identify the book (or article), the page number, and the sentences or illustrations so there is no question about what material you are referring to. Tell precisely why and how you want to use it. If you do not include enough detail, your request will be denied. See the example of a letter requesting permission on page 119.

Granting permission to use published material is not a high priority for publishers, and sometimes the publisher will have to contact the author before getting back to you. So, you may have to wait a couple of months for a response. If you are fortunate, you will be given permission to use the material. Usually, you will be required to give credit to the source of the quoted material. If you are requesting more than a few lines of text, an illustration, or lyrics, the publisher or author may require a fee from you. This fee may be minor or can range to $100 or more. You then have a choice of whether or not it is worth the cost to include the information.

Book and magazine titles, as well as ideas and concepts, cannot be copyrighted. A title makes up only a small portion of the text and therefore is excluded from copyright protection by the fair use policy. The copyright protects the author's particular arrangement of words, not ideas (with the exception of characters he or she creates). Therefore, you may rewrite another author's statements in your own words as long as you

Anita McIntyre
5748 Waterway Blvd.
Indianapolis, IN 46206
(317) 645-8334

March 5, 19—

Permissions Department
Houghton Mifflin Co.
228 Park Street
Boston, MA 02201

Dear Sir or Madam:

I am in the process of writing a book entitled *Indians of Arizona.* It is to be published by St. Martin's Press next fall. It describes the life, culture, and history of the native American Indians in Arizona. It will contain several dozen historical and contemporary drawings and photographs. This book will be distributed to bookstores, schools, and other appropriate markets throughout the United States.

I would like permission from you to use five paragraphs from a book published by your company. The book is entitled *Ancient American Cultures* by Lenord R. Rossen. The five paragraphs in question are found on pages 108 and 109 starting with the second paragraph. I have included photocopies of these pages with the text marked for your reference.

These paragraphs contain quotations from an interview with Chief Standing Elk, describing some of the ancient traditions of his people. This information, recorded in a colorful and descriptive style, conveys beautifully both the history and culture expressed in my book.

Thank you for considering my request and I look forward to your timely response.

Sincerely,

Anita McIntyre

A permissions letter.

do not paraphrase an entire work or a significant portion of it. If you cannot obtain permission to use some material or do not want to bother with the permissions process, you might consider restating the idea in your own words.

ILLUSTRATIONS

Illustrations include photographs, drawings, tables, diagrams, maps, graphs, and other visual material. With a few exceptions, it is the author's responsibility to obtain illustrations. Both book and magazine editors consider illustrations along with the text. Adding suitable illustrations can greatly enhance your manuscript, making it more useful and more saleable.

However, a book which requires too many illustrations may be less desirable to a publisher because they increase the production costs. Children's books sell best with many good illustrations, so it is important to have them. Most adult fiction, however, sells just as well without them. Adding illustrations would just increase publishing costs. Insisting on using color photos in your book will also scare publishers away. Color reproduction is so expensive that only a few types of books can be economically published with them. Leave this decision up to the publisher.

Publishers differ on how they like authors to present illustrations in their manuscripts. Some like them placed near the text, others like them clustered at the end of the manuscript. Captions or legends can be put on the back of each illustration or numbered and typed on a sheet of paper with the corresponding number written on each illustration. Some publishers prefer that each caption be placed on a separate sheet of paper. The publisher's author guidelines will tell you what is preferred. If they don't, or if the publisher does not have any specific guidelines, then the publisher is not that particular about how you present them, as long as they are properly identified and well organized. In that case, you will be okay if you follow the recommendations I provide in this section.

For magazine articles you can number each of the illustrations and type the captions on a separate sheet of paper. The publication will place the illustrations in the text as they see fit. For longer manuscripts you can list the illustrations at the end of each chapter or if you want to indicate an approximate position of the illustration, type in the text at the desired location "(Illustration x)". This annotation lets the editor know approximately where to place the illustration. It does not necessarily mean that the illustration will be placed in this exact spot in the text. Because space is determined by the page layout, it may be placed a suitable location nearby.

Photographs

Having photographs available is a definite advantage to you. If the editor knows that you have photos to accompany the manuscript, he is more likely to request to see your work. In fact, the availability of good photos may be the deciding factor that causes the editor to buy your manuscript.

If you don't have photos, or if the photos that you do have are unacceptable to the editor, the cost of obtaining them may be charged to you. This is usually the case with book publishers.

A magazine may stipulate that you include some publishable photos with your article in order to make the sale. They may even pay you extra for the photos.

You can shoot the photos yourself if you can produce *good quality* pictures. If not, hire a photographer or buy photos from a stock photo company (see Chapter 12). For black and white photos most editors prefer you use 8 x 10-inch glossy prints, but 5 x 7 may also be acceptable. If you need color photos, use 35 mm transparencies (commonly called slides), although color prints can be used if transparencies are not available.

You should not send photos with a query letter; just mention that they are available. If the publisher requests your manuscript, then you can send copies of the prints. Do not send your only copies, as they may get lost, and do not send negatives.

Identify each photo with your name, address, and phone number on the back. This will prevent the editor from accidentally mixing your photos with someone else's or misplacing them. Do not write on the back with a ball point pen as the pressure exerted by the pen may damage the face of the photos. Also, don't use a pen containing ink that might smear. I once received 120 photos from one author who had neatly identified each one and stacked them together. When I flipped through the photos I discovered that the ink on the back of each photo came off and ruined the face of the photo underneath. Almost all of his photos were useless and he had to reshoot them. Instead of writing the identification information on the back of the photo, I would suggest that you use a preprinted peel and stick label. You may also use a rubber stamp or a permanent marking pen, but make sure the ink is dry before stacking them.

Figure numbering and captions can be added by typing the information on a separate sheet of paper, cutting them out, and sticking them to the back of the photos.

Your caption should be descriptive in order to be useful. Avoid stating the obvious. If you have a picture of a farmer standing in front of his barn don't state, "A farmer standing in front of his barn." That is apparent from the photo. Give the reader some additional information that ties the picture to the text or adds additional information.

If you want to use a picture containing the likeness of someone that can be identified, you will probably need to get his or her written permission. You cannot assume that just because someone gave you permission to take a picture that you have the right to use it in any way you please. Verbal consent is not good enough. You should have the person sign a model release form. This is especially true for pictures that will be used for advertising or commercial purposes, which includes most books. Usually photos used for public educational purposes, such as newspapers, textbooks, encyclopedias, or magazines, do not need a model release, unless the photo is used as a cover illustration.

Model release forms will vary in style and content, but basically they give you the right to use the subject's likeness

MODEL RELEASE

I hereby irrevocably grant __________________ his/her heirs, legal representatives and assigns, those for whom photographer is acting, and those acting with his/her authority and permission, the right to copyright, in his/her own name or otherwise, and use photographic portraits or pictures of me, or in which I may be included in whole or in part, or composite or distorted in character or form, in conjunction with my own or a fictitious name, or reproductions thereof in color or otherwise, made through any media at his studios or elsewhere, for art advertising, trade, or any other lawful purpose. I also consent to the use of any printed matter in conjunction therewith.

I hereby waive any right that I may have to inspect and/or approve the finished product or the advertising copy that may be used in connection therewith, or the use to which it may be applied.

I hereby release, discharge, and agree to save photographer, his/her heirs, legal representatives and assigns, and all persons acting under his/her permission or authority or those for whom he/she is acting from any liability by virtue of any blurring, distortion, alteration, optical illusion, or use in composite form, whether intentional or otherwise, that may occur or be produced in the taking of said pictures, or in any processing rending towards the completion of the finished product.

Name______________________________Date____________

Address____

City/State/Zip______________________________________

Model's Signature___________________________________

Parent's or Guardian's Signature________________________

A model release form.

in the manner desired without the fear of demands for additional financial compensation or legal reprisals.

A sample of a model release form is shown on page 123. If the model is a minor, the signature of the parent or guardian is also required. If a fee was paid to the model, a clause stating such should be added. For example, "For the sum of $______, I hereby irrevocably grant..." Although most people are delighted at the possibility of having their likenesses published, some are not. Others, after publication, may change their minds or they might complain about the way the photo was cropped or reproduced. If each identifiable subject in your photos signs a release, you will avoid these problems. Additional examples of release forms can be found in *Photographer's Market* published by Writer's Digest Books and *Professional Business Practices in Photography* published by the American Society of Magazine Photographers.

When you send photos to your editor, include copies of the release forms.

Drawings

If drawings are needed most publishers prefer to commission their own. Some books are illustrated by the author, but most are not. Few writers have the artistic talent to create suitable drawings. Some writers have talented friends make drawings for them to submit with their manuscript. This is unnecessary. Unless you are a talented artist, your publisher will assign an artist to create the drawings that will accompany your work. Publishers prefer to use their own artists so they can match the manuscript with quality artwork created in an appropriate style.

If drawings are necessary for your manuscript, you may sketch them so the editor knows what drawings are needed. But it is usually best to let the publisher choose his own artist for the finished product. The publisher may charge you for the cost of producing the drawings. If the drawings comprise a major portion of the book, you may be expected to split the royalties with the artist.

CHAPTER 9

MAILING SUBMISSIONS

There is more to sending submissions than just putting them in the mail. If you do it the wrong way, you will be perceived as an amateur and will get the same treatment that most novice writers receive. If your submission is professionally prepared, don't allow it to be rejected just because it wasn't sent properly. In this chapter you will learn how to send materials to publishers and how to analyze and react to their responses.

ENVELOPES AND POSTAGE

When sending an editor your manuscript, use an envelope that is large and strong enough to hold it. If your manuscript is only five pages or less, you may fold it in thirds and send it in a #10 (business-size) envelope. For manuscripts over five pages, use 9 x 12-inch envelopes or larger.

When sending a manuscript, make sure you use the correct postage. I get envelopes stamped "Postage Due" much too frequently. These envelopes are sent back to the senders unopened.

If you want a response (either good or bad) from the publisher, you must include a self-addressed stamped envelope (SASE). Whether you are sending a one-page query letter or a full manuscript, you need to include a return envelope and postage. Some editors will not respond to you even if you do send a SASE simply because they are burdened with so many submissions. Most, however, will send you a reply if you have included a SASE. Even if you do not send a SASE, editors will respond if they are interested in seeing your material. For this reason, many writers do not send a SASE and just assume if the publisher does not respond after a certain amount of time, he is not interested.

Send an envelope large enough to accommodate the material you want returned, preaddressed, with stamps in place. If you are sending your material in a #10 envelope, send a business-size return envelope, folded in thirds. You could also use a slightly smaller #9 envelope which will fit into the #10 envelope without folding. If you are submitting material requiring a larger envelope, include an envelope large and sturdy enough to hold it.

You may decide that you don't need to have your manuscript returned. However, you still want to receive a response from the editor. If all you want is a response, all you need to send is a business-sized SASE. The manuscript, if not accepted, is then discarded. In your cover letter you may indicate that the manuscript need not be returned.

If you write to any publisher outside the country, you cannot use your country's postage stamps on your return envelopes. Stamps on the return envelope must be from the country from which it is to be mailed. A Canadian publisher, for example, must have Canadian stamps, which are difficult to find outside of Canada. What you can do is include an International Reply Coupon (IRC) with your envelope. You can purchase IRCs at any post office. The publisher exchanges them for postage at his post office. Postage rates are different in foreign countries, so make sure you buy enough IRCs for the return.

Since postage out of the country can be very expensive, especially for heavy manuscripts, it is best to send only a return envelope and postage and let the publisher keep the manuscript.

In place of sending a return envelope with a query letter or proposal, you might consider preparing a stamped self-addressed postcard. You can do this for publishers inside the country or out. Typed on one side can be the publisher's name and address with a list of pre-typed responses that allow the editor to merely check the appropriate response and drop it into the mail. An example of the responses listed might be as follows:

____Yes, I would be interested in seeing your manuscript.

____ No, I would not be interested at this time, but I would like to see material from you in the future.

____ No, I am not interested.

A postcard is the cheapest and quickest way to receive a response. The editor doesn't have to type and prepare a letter and envelope, and you save on postage.

If an editor requests a book proposal or your completed manuscript, mark on the outside of the envelope "Requested Proposal" or "Requested Manuscript." This way the editor and staff know that it isn't just another unsolicited submission to be thrown into the slush pile.

Your manuscripts can be sent in various ways. Overnight delivery is the quickest, but is usually unnecessary. First class mail (or Priority mail for packages over 12 ounces) or UPS ground service is suitable for most purposes. If you don't mind waiting a couple of extra weeks, you can send it by 4th class mail. Books and manuscripts can be sent 4th class at a substantially cheaper rate. The savings may only be a few dollars per mailing, but if you send your manuscript out to a lot of publishers, the cost will quickly add up. If you use 4th class, print "Return Postage Guaranteed" under your address to ensure that your package will be returned to you if it is undeliverable.

You might also consider using Certified or Registered mail if you are sending important documents, photos, tapes, or something of value. Certified mail requires the receiver to sign for it on its arrival. This provides you proof of delivery. Registered mail goes a step further by requiring a signature for every post office it passes through and can be traced if need be. Naturally, these services will cost you extra.

You might also insure the contents of your package, but this insurance is only payable on the tangible value of the material being sent. A manuscript could only be insured for the cost of the paper. So, unless you are sending something of value with the manuscript, it is best not to bother with insurance.

You may want to include photos with your manuscript. To prevent undue damage, reinforce your mailing envelope with cardboard inserts. Write on the outside of the envelope "PHOTOS—DO NOT BEND." You may also use a heavy cardboard envelope, available at packaging or photography supply stores.

Always make a copy of your manuscript, illustrations, and any documents that may accompany them. Once this material leaves your possession, you have no control over what happens to it. It may be lost or destroyed in the mail, misplaced by an editor, or accidentally thrown out by a member of the office staff.

RECORD KEEPING

Keep track of the queries, proposals, and manuscripts you send. Don't just sit back and wait for a response. Record what was sent (e.g., query, proposal, manuscript), date sent, who it was sent to (including editor's name and phone number), and enclosures (e.g., photos, documents). You should also find out the response time listed in *Writer's Market* and record this date.

Mail can be, and too frequently is, lost en route to its destination. In such cases you can wait forever without receiving a response. To eliminate this problem some authors include with the submission a self-addressed stamped postcard in addition to the return envelope. On receipt of the materials the editor is requested to return the postcard. This way the author knows that the editor actually received the submission.

On every self-addressed reply card or envelope you should put the return address of the publishing company. The reason for this is that not all editors will put their company name on the card. Also, companies change names or go through restructuring that alters their names, thus you may get a response with a different name on it or no name at all. If you write the company name on the envelope or card, you will know who it is from. If the company did change names, you can update your records.

When you receive a response, record the result and the date. This record is important. You may send out 50 or more packages before finding a publisher who will buy your material. If it takes that long, it doesn't mean your manuscript or your idea was bad, it just means that it took you longer than expected to find an editor savvy enough to recognize your manuscript's potential. Many books go through numerous rejections before finally being published, so don't give up!

Your record will show who has received your material, who is interested, who has rejected it, and who has declined it but invited further material from you in the future. I have received manuscripts/queries a second time after already rejecting them months earlier. I've also sent rejection letters in response to queries and still the authors send their manuscripts, thanking me for requesting their material. Keeping good records will help you avoid these mistakes.

Follow Up

If you sent a SASE, most publishers will send you a reply. If you have not received a response after the stated time has passed, write a follow-up letter politely inquiring about the status of your material. Address your follow-up letter to the same person to whom you submitted your material. If you only used the editor's title, without the name, your chances of a response are less likely. Your follow-up letter may say something like the following:

> On January 14th of this year, I submitted a manuscript entitled *How to Win at Hopscotch* for your consideration. It has been three months since the manuscript was sent, and I have not heard back from you. Would you please let me know what its status is at this time?
>
> I have enclosed a self-addressed stamped envelope for your convenience. Thank you for your time. I look forward to your reply.

Send a letter; don't call the editor on the phone! One thing busy editors can't stand is being annoyed by pesky authors. I receive more calls than I care to from authors who inquire about their manuscripts, to discuss the many virtues of their work, give me a sales pitch, or fill my ear with hype about how their book will be a bestseller. Its annoying and a waste of time. So please don't call the editor. Just send him a reminder. You certainly don't want to annoy your editor. He may bag your material just because he doesn't want to deal with you.

To make it easier for the editor to give you a reply, you may send a self-addressed stamped postcard. On the back of the card say something like this:

> On January 14th of this year, I submitted a manuscript entitled *How to Win at Hopscotch* for your consideration. It has been three months since the manuscript was sent and I have not heard back from you. Would you please mark the appropriate response on this card and return it to me? Thank you for your time.
>
> ____ Your material is still under consideration. We will be in touch with you soon.

____ We have no record of receiving your material. Please send it to us again.

____ We have reviewed your material and find it does not fit our current needs.

Comments:______________________________________
____

Don't forget to put the editor's company name and address in the return address corner of the envelope.

Record the date of your second letter and wait a few weeks. If you still don't receive a response, write another letter of inquiry. You might politely state that you will call in a few days to check with him. The warning of an annoying call could inspire him to respond quickly.

You don't want to sound threatening. Be polite and courteous. If he doesn't respond to your third letter in a few weeks, feel free to call. Chances are, if the editor has not responded to you by now, he is not interested in your material and will not reply. A phone call will probably do little good and may be screened by a secretary anyway. Some editors won't respond to any submission from an unfamiliar author unless they are interested in the material, even if it does contain a SASE. In that case, repeated inquires or phone calls won't do any good.

Any editor who requests your manuscript owes you a response. You should keep in contact with him until you receive one.

If you didn't send a SASE with an unsolicited query or manuscript, you probably will not receive a response *unless* the editor is interested in your material. If you did send a return envelope, most editors will respond within the reported time frame.

Taxes

Besides the records of your submissions, you need to keep records for tax purposes. Even if you haven't sold anything yet, when you do, you will need to have an account of all of your expenses.

What can you deduct? Any expenses related to creating and selling your work: postage, paper, stationery, typing or other services, travel expenses, gasoline usage, phone, etc. Any expense undertaken to create your work is legitimate. If you have an office in your home exclusively set aside for your writing, you can deduct a portion of your rent or mortgage. In order to do this, though, the room must be used exclusively for your business and nothing else. For further information on what you can deduct, I highly recommend that you go to your local IRS office and pick up their publications *Tax Guide for Small Business* (Publication 334) and *Business Use of Your Home* (Publication 587).

Keep a file and put all of your receipts in it. You must have proof for each expense you claim as a deduction. If you are ever audited, you will be required to produce your receipts. Keep these records for a least three years for audits can go back that far. Keep a journal and a file. Write down expenses and payments received. Get receipts for everything, including credit card receipts.

REJECTION LETTERS

Your most common response from editors will be rejection letters. All writers receive rejections. It comes with the job. Even the big name authors who have works on the bestseller lists have received rejections. They didn't give up after their first, second, or third rejection. So don't get discouraged.

Although every rejection letter (or card) is different, they say basically the same thing. A typical form letter might read:

> Thank you for contacting us about your proposed book. We have carefully reviewed the material you submitted to us; unfortunately, it is not the type of project we are looking for at this time.

> We appreciate your interest in our company and wish you the best of luck in placing your work with another publisher.

Because editors send so many rejections, they rely on form letters to save time. If, by chance, you receive a rejection that obviously was not a form letter, you should look at this as something special. The editor took the time to give you some encouragement or perhaps even invite you to submit to her in the future. The fact that she didn't have to do this says that, although your current manuscript may not be of interest, she thought enough of your writing to invite you to submit material to her again in the future. This is encouraging. A form letter gives no evaluation of your manuscript. Unless the editor accepts your work, you will not get any recommendations or suggestions on how to improve your material. You are simply told "no thanks." A personal letter says "good job—try again."

Keep these editors on file. When you write your next manuscript, they should be among the first ones you should send it to. Now that you have had some communication with them, they are not total strangers. In your cover letter you might remind them that they had invited you to submit material to them. This statement will make the editor much more receptive and she won't treat it like a cold solicitation. You've got the editor's attention and she will consider your proposal more seriously.

CHAPTER 10

LITERARY AGENTS

In this book you have learned how to prepare and submit your work to publishers. This is also one of the major duties of a literary agent. If you can do this job yourself, you don't really need an agent. Most agents won't do anything different than what I have told you to do. However, many publishing houses, particularly the larger companies, require all submissions to be sent in by agents, so you will need an agent if you want to approach them. You might also want to consider using an agent if you do not want to spend the time sending submissions or feel that you need help negotiating a publishing agreement.

If your primary interest is writing magazine articles, forget about using an agent. Most agents concentrate on book-length manuscripts only. The money earned from magazine articles, as well as short stories and poetry, is usually not enough for them to bother with. A few agents do handle articles and other short pieces, but only for well-known authors seeking publication in the largest and highest paying magazines.

Send an agent the same type of material you would send to a publisher. Most agents prefer to receive a query letter or book proposal before seeing the complete manuscript. Like publishers, they are bombarded with submissions. Some agents receive so many submissions that they will not even return self-addressed stamped envelopes unless they are impressed by an author's work.

Writers who have not learned the secrets of getting published, as I have described in this book, will find it hard to locate a good agent willing to work with them. Good agents will not work with just any writer. The writer must have a saleable product and show some degree of professionalism. If you want to work with an agent and you have a marketable manuscript, by following the recommendations I have outlined in this book you will find an agent.

HOW AGENTS WORK

Writers should always send agents a query letter first. If the agent is interested in working with the author, he will request additional material. When an agent finds a manuscript he feels has publishing potential, he will accept it for representation. The author is then sent a contract or letter of agreement specifying the agent's commission, fees, and other terms of representation. When that document is signed and returned, the agent begins seeking suitable publishers to purchase the rights to the manuscript.

The agent sends out query letters or book proposals only to those companies that might have an interest in the material he is trying to sell. As you learned in previous chapters, all publishers have specific interests and focus on certain types of books. Agents should know what publishers want. This information is given in directories like *Writer's Market* and *Novel and Short Story Writer's Market,* and agents become very familiar with them. When a publisher shows interest, terms are negotiated and the publisher draws up the contract, which is signed by the author and agent.

Literary agents are paid a 10 to 20 percent commission on sales they make, 15 percent being the most common for sales within the country and 20 percent for sales outside the country. The commission is paid on all royalties earned by the author, including the advance. The publisher will send the royalty check to the agent, who then deducts his commission and forwards the rest to the author.

It is in the agent's best interest to get as large a royalty as possible, but royalties are not the only consideration. Advances are equally important, especially from the large publishing companies. Advances are part of the royalty paid to the author before the book is available for sale. Typically they are paid in two installments: the first after the contract is signed and the second when the completed manuscript is delivered and accepted by the publisher. Most agents will try to get as large an advance as possible so that if the book fails to earn more than the advance amount, the agent and author come out ahead. Considering the failure rate of new books, this is an important concern.

A good agent can work wonders for an author with a highly marketable manuscript. Agents, however, aren't expected to be magicians. They cannot sell unsaleable manuscripts. They also do not normally edit manuscripts, although they may offer this service separately. Usually they leave the editing up to the author and publisher, although they will often offer suggestions and advice on improving manuscripts.

Some agents may request that your manuscript be read by a freelance editor or proofreader before it is sent out to publishers. Agents can perform this service themselves, or refer clients to freelancers. In most cases, editing will not only improve the manuscript, but greatly improve the chances of having the work accepted for publication. The author-agent relationship can be a mutually beneficial arrangement. This is particularly true for writers who have excellent material to sell and want to get the most they can from the largest publishing companies.

ADVANTAGES OF WORKING WITH AN AGENT

There are advantages and disadvantages to working with a literary agent. Let's first discuss some of the positive aspects of using an agent.

A good agent can open doors for you and get your material in front of editors who would otherwise never see it. You will need an agent to approach the large publishing companies.

Publishers are bombarded with unsolicited manuscripts. Overworked editors do not want to spend time digging through all of this material, so unsolicited manuscripts end up in slush pile. Here they will remain until they are sent back to the author or until an editor with some spare time rummages through them. Since editors have little spare time, this material gets little attention. Most big companies won't even consider looking at unsolicited material. Having an agent represent you is about the only way to bring your material to their attention.

Having material submitted by an agent usually keeps it from ending up in the slush pile and puts it into the hands of an appropriate editor. Publishers like to work with agents because agents screen the material, saving the editor the trouble of searching through a stack of manuscripts. Agents weed out all undesirable manuscripts, submitting only those that have marketing potential, are well-written, and would be of interest to the publisher. When material is submitted by an agent, editors are much more inclined to give it adequate attention.

Successful agents often are on a first name basis with many editors and can personally recommend a client's manuscript. This often proves more effective than just sending a query letter because the agent can convey his enthusiasm for the work.

For these reasons, publishers give the material submitted by agents preferential attention. If you have a competent agent working for you, then you know your material will get serious consideration. Agents also will be able to tap into markets with which you may be unfamiliar with, such as obtaining magazine rights, television and movie rights, and foreign publication rights. In most cases an agent can negotiate a more favorable contract than the author can. For exceptional manuscripts, agents can start a bidding war, with the manuscript going to the highest bidder. The final outcome results in increased revenue for the author, which may more than pay for the agent's commission.

THE COST OF REPRESENTATION

Literary agents receive more compensation than just the commissions from their clients' books. Additional fees reimburse them for their expenses. Other fees pay them for extra services they provide to the author. Some are paid simply to read authors' manuscripts. You should be aware of all the fees you may be asked to pay.

Established literary agents, like publishers, are flooded with unsolicited manuscripts. They spend most of their time reading, rather than marketing, books. Although they may be representing 20 or 30 different clients at a time, not all of the manuscripts they work with will get published. Because of this, many agents supplement their commission income by charging fees to authors. Some agents require fees from unpublished writers only. Some agents charge a marketing or consulting fee to all clients to cover the cost of postage and telephone expenses. Since most new writers are not lucky enough to get published, the chances that an agent will sell a novice writer's material are not good. Many of the old, well established literary agencies and agents will not consider representing unpublished authors. Agents who are willing to work with unpublished authors often charge a fee as compensation for their time and effort.

Many agents offer consultation services, which are available to anybody whether they are clients or not. Authors who have a manuscript sold without the help of an agent can pay for advice on negotiating contracts. These fees range from $20-$200 per hour.

Many agents will also charge a reading fee. The fee can vary anywhere from $40 to $300 or more. This is a fee the author pays just to have the agent read the manuscript. It is paid to the agent as compensation for the time spent in reading, not for representation. The agent is not expected to evaluate the manuscript or make any suggestions on improvement. It is just a payment for reading the manuscript. If the agent feels the manuscript can be sold, he will offer to represent the author and attempt to sell it. Whether he accepts the manuscript or not, the agent still is paid the reading fee. Often agents will refund the reading fees if they are able to make a sale. Some agents will accept almost any manuscript offered to them and charge a large reading fee (also called a representation or consulting fee). Some of the less successful agents make most of their money this way.

Another fee commonly charged by some literary agents is a criticism fee, which can range up to $400 or more. It involves not only reading the manuscript, but writing a detailed evaluation or critique for the author. In this sense, the agent also functions as a literary critic.

Most of the older or more established literary agencies do not charge their clients reading fees. However, they are also much more selective and will not represent any writer unless he or she has already had several books published. Therefore, most new authors are restricted to working with agents who are willing to take a risk, but who will also probably charge a reading fee.

Almost all agents charge a marketing fee, as it is frequently called. This fee covers the expense of marketing the author's material. It includes postage, phone and fax, photocopying, express mail expenses, and the like. A set amount, such as $20 or $40, might be charged for each book the agent represents, or instead of charging a set fee, he may bill the author for these expenses as they occur.

PUBLISHING AGREEMENTS

Except for the advance, the terms of a publishing contract do not vary much from house to house or author to author. Even a contract offered to new writers will not vary much from the one they offer to established authors.

Unless you have an extraordinary book, as an unpublished author you will have little bargaining power. You will probably have to take what you are offered. Sometimes when the publisher offers a new writer a contract, he will recommend that you get an agent. Once your book has been accepted for publication, finding an agent to represent you will be easy. Since you have already found a publisher, all the agent has to do is negotiate the contract for you.

An experienced agent knows which terms can be negotiated, and what ones are worth negotiating. In that respect he can be helpful, but an agent really isn't necessary. The thought of negotiating a publishing agreement, let alone understanding it, can be frightening to some people. Contracts in general are notoriously confusing, being overloaded with legal talk unfamiliar to most of us. Luckily, you don't need to be a lawyer to understand a book contract, although if you've never seen one before, you may be slightly confused.

Publishing agreements aren't difficult to understand if you have someone explain them to you. I won't spend much time on contracts here because it would take an entire book to explain them adequately. Instead, I will recommend two excellent books on the subject, written in layman's language. The books are *How to Understand and Negotiate a Book Contract or Magazine Agreement* and *A Writer's Guide to Contract Negotiations*, both written by Richard Balkin. The books pull apart some publishing agreements and explain them section by section. They also explain the negotiating process and how to deal with a publisher to get the best possible terms. After reading either of these books, you will have a good, basic understanding of publishing agreements and be able to intelligently read and negotiate your own contracts.

If you receive a publishing offer without the aid of an agent and do not plan to use an agent but have questions about the contract, you can get free legal advice from the Volunteer Lawyers for the Arts. They offer this service to authors of modest income. There are some thirty offices throughout the United States and Canada. For more information, contact:

Volunteer Lawyers for the Arts
1285 Avenue of the Americas
3rd Floor
New York, NY 10019
(212) 977-9270

DO YOU NEED AN AGENT?

With the knowledge you have gained from reading this book, you should be able to approach most publishers without using an agent. You will only need an agent to approach the largest publishing companies.

Even though most large and medium-sized publishing companies refuse to accept unsolicited manuscripts, you *can* approach them. Unsolicited does not necessarily mean unagented. What it means is that they do *not* want your first contact with them to be your manuscript. They prefer to receive a query letter first. Then if they ask to see your material, it becomes a solicited manuscript. By initially contacting them with a professionally prepared query letter your material will be given the same consideration as one coming from a published author or agent. And you will avoid being rejected simply for sending in an unrequested manuscript.

If you are a published author with several successful books to your credit, an agent might be helpful to you. Successful agents are always looking for successful authors to work with. These agents are frequently on a first name basis with editors and can pitch your book more effectively to them. And, of course, agents know how to negotiate contracts. The problem is that most of these agents do not work with new writers. They handle only authors who have already had some success getting published. Most agents who are willing to work with unpublished writers are also less experienced or less successful. They cannot do as much for an unpublished author. Publishers are less willing to negotiate contracts on works from new authors, and most agents do not have personal contacts with the publishing companies (especially if they are not located in New York). So, if you are an unpublished author you may be better off trying to get your own work published. But if your work is of professional quality, has great marketing potential, and a *good* agent is willing to represent you, you can definitely benefit from an author-agent relationship.

HOW TO FIND A GOOD AGENT

There are many advantages to using agents, especially if you want to be published by the larger publishing houses. Small publishers don't care if a manuscript is sent in by an agent or the author. Most of the authors who are published by smaller companies are not represented by an agent. Some authors have found that they can do a better job without an agent. There are good agents and there are agents who are not so good. A poor agent can be a waste of time and a needless expense to you.

As a publisher, I receive material submitted by many different agents. Frankly, I am surprised by the number of people calling themselves agents who do not know how to properly prepare and submit manuscripts or query letters. I find that some of them know less about getting published than many authors. These types of agents are doing their clients more harm than good. If you decide to work with an agent, be careful. Choose one that has been in the business for some time, can provide you with trade references, can show you a listing of publishers to whom they have recently sold books, and can refer you to satisfied clients. If an agent won't give you this information, be cautious. Some good, well-known, and busy agencies may not respond to all of these questions, but they should have a listing of recently sold books.

Beware of an agent who sold a manuscript to some large well-known publisher three or four years ago but has not sold anything recently. Successful agents should be making sales continually. If they aren't, they may be making their livings off of the fees they charge their clients rather than from commissions. You don't want to work with this type of agent.

Many writers complain that getting a good agent is almost impossible unless you are already a successfully published author. This is one reason why so many new writers end up working with incompetent agents. Novice or inexperienced agents are willing to work with just about anybody or with any type of book. Most good agents specialize in certain types of books. An agent who is willing to represent any book is not an experienced professional. Some large agencies handle many different types of books, assigning individual agents to handle each genre. That is why these agents are successful—they know their fields of specialty.

Don't get suckered into working with an agent just because he claims that your book is "fantastic" or a potential "bestseller"; he may just be buttering you up. And be careful with agents who emphasize fees or try to charge fees other than those I've mentioned in this chapter.

Because good literary agents receive hundreds of manuscripts, you may put in as much work trying to find an agent interested in your work as you would in trying to find a publisher.

So, how do you find a competent agent? The best way to find an agent is through personal contacts. Ask friends or colleagues who are published writers, for their agent's name. Many agents, in fact, will not consider taking on new clients unless they have been recommended by an existing client, so it works both ways.

Another place to look is in directories which list literary agencies. Four of the best sources include *Literary Market Place, Literary Agents of North America, International Writers' and Artists' Yearbook,* and *Guide to Literary Agents and Art/Photo Reps.* Your local library should have one or more of these books on its shelves. These directories contain hundreds of agents who are located all across North America as well as some foreign countries. Most writers go to one of these directories in search of an agent.

Writers' magazines often contain advertisements from literary agents looking for new clients. Since most agents receive more inquires than they can comfortably handle, an agent that spends money to advertise should be approached with caution.

Literary agents learn their trade by experience. Many are successful authors themselves or former editors. A few work their way up the ranks in established agencies. Literary agents are not required to have any special training or accreditation; however, membership in one of two trade organizations requires them to adhere to a code of ethics and standards, giving them some degree of recognition as professionals. The major organization for agents is the Association of Authors' Representatives (which, by the way, prohibits most of its members from charging reading fees). A second organization, Writer's Guild of America (WGA), has many agents as members. Agents can become members of the WGA by signing the Guild's agreement on basic standards for the treatment of writers.

Most good agents are members of at least one of these organizations. You can get a list of members by writing to these organizations and requesting a membership listing. A fee may be required, but it should be no more than a few of dollars. The addresses for these organizations can be found in the Appendix.

For additional information on literary agents I recommend reading *Literary Agents: A Writer's Guide* by Debby Mayer, and *Literary Agents: How to Get and Work With the Right One for You* by Michael Larsen. Written from the author's perspective, these books provide interesting and valuable information about literary agents and how they work.

Another Success Story

For five years mystery lover Sara Paretsky had been thinking about writing her own novel. Unlike the dozens of mysteries she had read, Paretsky wanted to use a hard-boiled female detective. With encouragement from a friend, Paretsky signed up for a class on "Writing the Detective Novel" at a local university. The instructor, Stuart Kaminsky, was the author of the popular Toby Peters mystery series.

Kaminsky's professional criticism helped Paretsky develop her writing style and polish her manuscript. It took Paretsky a year and a half to finish her first book *Indemnity Only* featuring private eye V.I. Warshawski. Impressed with her work, Kaminsky introduced her to his own agent. The agent did not have immediate success with her book. He approached 14 publishers before selling it to Dial Press.

The strong female character in Paretsky's story was a departure from other detective fiction at the time. V.I. Warshawski was a mixture of toughness and vulnerability. She could bring down an antagonist with a well placed punch and out-think clever crooks, yet she had a passion for fine cooking and designer clothing.

Indemnity Only became the first of a series of mysteries which includes the bestselling *Burn Marks* and *Guardian Angel* and led to the making of a movie starring Kathleen Turner as V.I. Warshawski.

Paretsky's books, although successful, did not bring her great wealth. It wasn't until her fifth book that she was able to make enough money to live on.

As an inexperienced novelist, she gained familiarity with words on the job writing newsletters and brochures. Writing newsletters she says, "May not tax your creativity but it exercises your writing muscle."

Writing, however, didn't come naturally to Paretsky; she had to work at it. "Words very seldom come easily," she says. "It's always a long, slow, painful process." When writing *Guardian Angel* she said, "I would get up at 5 a.m. and start writing. I wrote until I just couldn't do it anymore, physically. My hands would give out." It took almost two years to finish.

As with all of her books, Paretsky researches and finds background information, examines buildings and neighborhoods so she can accurately describe them in her stories.

The characters in her books experience the same struggles of daily life she is familiar with. "I have to see my characters as real people and be able to imagine them in the situation. It's a process of emotional identification."

For individual scenes she says, "I try to feel what I would be feeling if I were in a particular situation. If I were in a burning building, I feel my palms tingling, I feel the hairs on the back of my neck starting to rise. I'm in the situation physically. Mentally, I decide what is happening, too. Am I getting angry? Am I reflectively holding back? Is my heart beating faster?"

After putting the story down on paper Paretsky says, "I begin the agonizing process of rewriting that seems to be so necessary."

Paretsky's preparation and dedication to perfecting each book has made her a successful author.

CHAPTER 11

ALTERNATIVE BOOK MARKETS

In this book you have learned about the standard markets where you can sell your writing. There are several additional markets where books can be sold. If you have not had success with commercial publishers, either small or large, you might consider approaching some of these markets. In fact, your manuscript may be better suited for one of the alternative markets.

BOOK PRODUCERS

Book producers offer authors an alternative way of getting their work into print. Although originally known as "book packagers," most companies prefer to be called book producers or book developers. A book producer develops and prepares books to sell to publishers. Book producers can develop ideas in-house or accept submissions from outside writers. They may perform any function from writing the manuscript (or assigning a writer to do it), preparing the text and illustrations, to even publishing the book.

Usually a book producer will start with a proposal. If a publisher shows interest, the producer will prepare the manuscript, copyedit, design the page layout, incorporate illustrations, typeset the text, design a book cover, and deliver it to the publisher ready for printing. The degree of work the producer undertakes on each book is negotiated with the publisher.

Many publishers like to work with book producers because producers supply publishers with completed books ready for publication without tying up their own employees. Publishers with small staffs can rely on book producers to provide them with books they would not have time to develop themselves. Publishers can also add books to their lines in subject areas where their resources or editorial expertise are limited.

Authors should approach book producers just as they would a publisher. Many of them are listed in directories such as *Writer's Market.* Like publishers, they have areas of specialization. Send each one a query, proposal, or manuscript as indicated in *Writer's Market.* If they see potential in your work, they will have you sign a packaging agreement with them.

If a book producer contacts an author to write a manuscript, payment is usually a set fee. If the book producer accepts an unassigned submission from an author, he will either pay a flat fee or a royalty. Publishers will offer book producers a royalty one or two percent higher than what they offer authors to compensate for expenses incurred while preparing the book for publication. The book producer, in turn, will offer the author some percentage of the publisher's royalty, as much as 50 percent or more, or as low as 10 percent. This may seem like the author is giving away a lot to the book producer, but he really is not. He is paying the book producer for some very valuable services. The book producer will spend thousands of dollars and many hours preparing the author's manuscript. The manuscript will be polished and professional-looking. Without the packager's help, the manuscript might never have been published, not necessarily because it was not marketable, but because the competition for publication is so fierce, a book must be better than the competition. Having the manuscript packaged as a book gives it a definite advantage over all the other submissions and saves the publisher time and money.

Your royalties from a book producer will not be as good as those directly from a publisher, but any royalty may be better than none at all. It also gets your work into print, giving you a valuable writing credit and an inside track to the publishing company who bought your work.

There are well over a hundred packagers in the United States. Most book producers, however, are not interested in publishing a writer's proposed manuscript. They are more interested in finding writers who can produce the manuscripts they have in development. If, for instance, a publisher is interested in a book on motorcycle racing, the packager will seek out a writer with experience in that area.

Those book producers who accept submissions from authors are listed in *Writer's Market* after the Book Publishers listings. A more complete listing of all book producers can be found in *Literary Market Place*.

UNIVERSITY PRESSES

Another market which you might consider is the university press. There are approximately a hundred university presses in the United States. Most of their funding is subsidized by the government, private foundations, and other groups. When funding is not available from these sources, the author may be asked to contribute to the cost of publication.

Contrary to what many people may think, university presses do not publish just textbooks and class manuals. In fact, they leave most of that up to textbook publishers. University presses publish on a wide range of topics of both general and specialized interest. Topics include history, biography, politics, education, religion, science, business, economics, geography, poetry, and fiction, to mention just a few. Most have a strong interest in regional titles.

Here is a representative sample of titles published by university presses:

Alexander to Actium: The Historical Evolution of the Hellenistic Age
Dysfunctionalism in Afrikan Education
Agriculture in Sierra Leone
The Letters of Rudyard Kipling
Greek Tragedy and Its Legacy
Law, Ethics and the Visual Arts
The Dictionary of American Bird Names
The Collected Poems of Henri Coulette
Crazeology: The Autobiography of a Chicago Jazzman
Starting A Small Restaurant
The Teenager's Guide to the Best Summer Opportunities
How to Take Great Trips with Your Kids
The Citrus Cookbook

This list shows the wide variety of topics published by university presses. Some are academic, while others are similar to any other popular book that may be found in a bookstore.

University presses, more than other publishers, will consider publishing material simply because of its literary quality and value. Unlike commercial publishers, the university presses' main goal is not to make a profit or to find bestsellers. They are not focused on finding books with mass appeal or big potential sales. University presses will consider, on merit, almost any subject of scholarly interest. They look for evidence of original research, use of reliable sources, clarity of organization, and complete development of the theme with documentation and supportive footnotes or bibliography. They want books that will make significant contributions to knowledge in the fields treated.

If they think a book has merit, it has a chance of being published. Sometimes, if the book appears to have limited marketing potential and outside funding is not available, the publisher will offer to produce a limited number of the books under a subsidy arrangement with the author. This means the author will be expected to pay part or all of the printing cost. Although university presses are not focused toward making huge profits, they do need to pay for expenses. Developing, producing, and selling books cost money. Usually the author on a subsidy arrangement will pay some portion of the cost to get the book published. Since huge sales are not expected, the print run will be small and the cost to the author relatively low. The amount could vary anywhere from a few hundred to several thousand dollars.

University presses are respected in the book industry and produce top quality products. Their books are sold to all book outlets including bookstores, libraries, schools, department stores, and elsewhere.

Writer's Market lists university presses in its main book section along with most other commercial publishers. Because money is not the focal point of their publishing program, they offer low advances, if any at all. The average print run for their books is typically 1,000 to 2,000 copies. Most of their books (95-99 percent) are submitted by the author without the aid of an agent. University presses are very receptive to new authors because the work is judged by its merits, not by its marketing potential.

SUBSIDY PUBLISHING

In addition to university presses there are many other publishers which subsidize their publishing. Some of these companies are almost indistinguishable from commercial publishers. Others operate entirely as subsidy presses and are distinctly different in operation and purpose from the publishers discussed so far in this book.

Commercial publishing companies involved in subsidy publishing get their funds from private and government organizations and foundations just like university presses, as well as from the authors. These presses, like university presses, feel an obligation to produce quality or scholarly works even though the financial rewards may not be great. When an author is asked to share in the cost of producing his or her book, it is often termed co-publishing. Companies involved in co-publishing are primarily commercial publishers. Their subsidy programs comprise no more than 50 percent of their publishing program, and usually much less.

A publisher may offer to co-publish a book with an author if the book fits his line but has a limited market. For example, a publisher who has a strong line of pet books may ask a writer to share in the production costs for a book on a rare breed of dog. The publisher will actively market the book along with all of his other books and pay the author a typical royalty of 5-15 percent. Sometimes the publisher may request that the royalties start only after 1,000 or 2,000 books have sold, in order to compensate him for his expenses. This could be instead of the author's subsidy, or in addition to it. The amount charged for co-publication is typically $2,000-$5,000. If you have a specialized book with a limited market or can't get published otherwise, co-publishing is a legitimate option to consider. Co-publication provides an opportunity for authors to get their works published by a respectable company.

There are other publishers whose publishing programs consist almost entirely of author subsidized books. These commercial subsidy presses are often referred to as "vanity" presses because they satisfy the author's need of seeing his or her book in print. Vanity presses are distinctly different from publishers who are involved in co-publishing as described above.

Most people in the book industry have little respect for vanity presses. There are, however, both advantages and disadvantages of working with a vanity press. Let me point out the positive aspects first.

The primary advantage of using a vanity press is that they will publish any book offered to them, as long as it does not contain material which is libelous, obscene, or otherwise illegal. Many authors who have exhausted all normal channels of getting their work published turn to subsidy publishing. These authors either have a great deal of faith in the value of their work, or simply want to satisfy their egos. A few books published this way have become moderately successful despite being rejected by other publishers.

Another positive aspect of vanity publishing is that most commercial subsidy presses will do a good job of preparing your manuscript for publication and will produce a nice looking book. They have graphic artists who will lay out the text and illustrations and will create a pleasing book cover. The finished volume will be equal in appearance to any book found in the bookstore. The author can take pride in its appearance and feel a sense of accomplishment.

Royalties from vanity presses are usually significantly larger than for other publishers. While most publishers will pay a royalty of about 5-15 percent, vanity presses will pay up to 40 percent. They do this in an attempt to convince the author that he or she will eventually be compensated for putting money up front to produce the book.

Working with a vanity press can sound enticing. They will accept almost any manuscript, produce a good looking book, and pay the author an enormous royalty on every copy sold. These points are stressed in their sales literature. What they don't adequately explain are the many drawbacks associated with their form of subsidized publishing.

The cost is one of the biggest drawbacks. The author will be expected to pay anywhere from $5,000 to $25,000, depending on the size and complexity of the book. An average-sized book will cost about $15,000.

The printing usually consists of no more than 500 books.* Even though the author pays for these books, they belong to the publisher and not the author. The author will be given a

---

*Although some vanity publishers may claim to publish as many as 1000 books, they may print the pages for this many, but will only bind and complete 500 copies. It is rare for a vanity press to sell more than this amount. If, by chance, they do sell the initial 500 copies, they would then bind the remaining pages.

dozen or so copies free of charge. If he wants any additional copies, he must pay for them again.

At a cost of $15,000 for 500 books, the author ends up paying about $30 for each one. The publisher must price the books to be competitive to other books, so the retail price will probably be far less than $30. Which means, that even if the publisher sold all of the copies at full retail price, the author would not get back the entire amount paid.

The fee charged to authors not only covers the printing cost, but expenses incurred in preparing the book for publication and marketing, and a substantial profit for the publisher. Vanity presses make their profit not from the sale of books, but from the fees charged to the author. They don't expect to make any money from the sales of their books. For this reason, their marketing efforts are very limited. According to their publishing contracts with their authors, they are committed to do some very basic marketing and publicity, but nothing more. This usually consists of sending out a few copies of the book to reviewers, listing the book in the publisher's catalog, and announcing the book's publication in a few published sources, which are available to all publishers.

Because vanity presses will publish just about anything, no matter how unmarketable or poorly written, they have a bad reputation within the book industry. Although they will edit the books, the editing is very shallow—correcting only obvious spelling and grammatical errors. They will not rewrite the text or do much in the way of correcting confusing or improperly constructed sentences. If the manuscript was hard to read, the book will be the same. Since the vast majority of the material they publish was rejected by other publishers and generally considered unpublishable, their books are looked upon as substandard. Book reviewers shun them and book dealers avoid them; consequently sales are extremely poor. The president of Vantage Press, the country's largest vanity publisher, once stated that perhaps as many as five percent of the books his company publishes each year will make a profit. This means at least 95 percent of the books they publish are financial failures for the authors, even though they may receive a 40 percent royalty.

Chances are the publisher will never sell the initial 500 books published, so the author will not even recover expenses, let alone make a profit.

As I have shown, there are a few advantages to vanity publishing, but for most authors the disadvantages far outweigh them. The majority of authors write in hopes of making a profit. If this is your primary reason for getting your work published, do not use a vanity press. However, there are times when subsidy publishing is useful and a viable choice. If your desire for publication is not motivated by profit, and other options are not available, subsidy publishing can be beneficial.

Some people subsidize their work not in hopes of making a profit or seeing their names in print, but to produce a volume that would be of benefit to a small number of people. Family histories, genealogical records, memoirs, and such fit into this category. Only family or close friends would have an interest in these books. Scholarly works with little appeal outside a certain academic community might also be published in this manner. A detailed analysis of the handwritten, first-draft version of James Joyce's *Ulysses*, is one example.

Of course, if your primary reason for wanting to get published is the pride of seeing your book in print, a subsidy press will satisfy that desire too.

Subsidy presses are listed at the end of the book section in *Writer's Market.* All publishers involved in co-publishing, even if only a small percentage of their books are subsidized, are listed here. Companies whose publishing programs consist of 50 percent or more author subsidized books (vanity publishers) are listed by name only after this section.

SELF-PUBLISHING

If you have a book you feel is well-written and has marketing potential, you might consider self-publishing. Many people who have been repeatedly rejected by commercial publishers have found success by doing it on their own.

As part of a fundraising project, Vicki Lansky wrote a cookbook called *Feed Me, I'm Yours*, which consisted of nutritional recipes for babies. With encouragement from family and friends she sought to have it published. After receiving 49 rejections she was discouraged. However, she knew the book was good and would be beneficial to others, so she decided to publish it herself. Even with no prior experience in publishing, her book became a bestseller. Lansky sold 300,000 copies of the original edition before selling paperback rights to Bantam, who went on to sell another half million copies. The book is still in print after nearly 20 years, and continues to sell well.

Lansky had a book with great potential, but none of the publishers she approached recognized it. Only through self-publication was she able to prove its value. In the process she made a handsome profit and embarked on an exciting new career.

Some other bestselling books that were originally self-published include: *What Color is Your Parachute?*, *Mary Ellen's Book of Helpful Hints*, *The One Minute Manager*, *Roberts Rules of Order*, *Bartlett's Familiar Quotations*, *How to Flatten Your Stomach*, and *How to Keep Your Volkswagen Alive*. Like the authors of these books, if you have a good, marketable product you can be successful.

There are some distinct advantages to self-publishing. You have complete control over the editing of your book, its appearance, and how it is marketed. Some authors know who their potential audience is better than a publisher does, and can promote a book in ways and in places unfamiliar to the publisher. A self-publisher can exploit these markets and reap all the rewards.

Let's look at a couple of hypothetical examples of the profit potential in self-publishing. Most books published these days sell in the range of $10-$25. Let's say you self-publish a book and you sell it for $15. Like most authors, you believe your book is a bestseller and you end up selling a million copies. Your gross revenue would come to $15,000,000. This is not all profit, you will have expenses to pay. But even if you deduct

80 percent of this amount to account for expenses, it leaves you with an income of three million dollars! Not bad. Of course, not all books are million-copy bestsellers. But even if you only sold 100,000 copies and deducted 80 percent for expenses, you would be left with $300,000. Makes self-publishing sound enticing doesn't it?

Many service companies, such as graphic designers, typesetters, printers, consultants, and others encourage people to self-publish in an effort to sell their services to them. You see many advertisements expounding the benefits of self-publishing in magazines, all aimed at enticing you to use the advertiser's services. With the development of desktop publishing, some people talk about self-publishing as the money making opportunity of the future.

With all this hype, many people are enticed into self-publishing, only to be disappointed. The facts are that very few people can make a profit self-publishing. Publishing is a very risky venture. A commercial publisher has more failures than successes, but because he publishes many books, the successful ones offset his losses. Publishing a single book is a high-risk undertaking, especially if you have no prior publishing experience.

The vast majority of self-publishers end up in debt and with a garage full of unsold books. The cost of preparing and producing a thousand copies of a 250-page book can easily amount to $5,000 or more. Advertising, publicity, and promotion can add several thousand more to that. If you do not have the cash to invest (and possibly lose) in this type of project, you shouldn't self-publish.

Besides the expense, self-publishing involves hundreds of important functions that require a great deal of time and effort. You will need to do all the editing, text design, and layout. You must create a commercially competitive book cover, register the book with appropriate government and private agencies, and find a printer. You will be responsible for storage, packing and shipping orders, invoicing and collections, and handling returns (which may amount to 50 percent or more from book dealers). You must constantly promote your book and seek out new markets. You could easily spend far more time publishing and marketing your book than you did writing it.

If you have never published a book before, you will also need to spend time learning how to perform all of these functions correctly. You could hire others to help you accomplish many of these jobs, but this will cost money and may make an otherwise moderately successful venture unprofitable.

Most self-publishers, after writing their books and getting them published, have no idea how to sell them. You can't just go down to the local bookstore and ask them if they want to stock your book. It doesn't work that easily. Most book dealers refuse to stock self-published books. One reason is because many of them "look" self-published. If your book is not on a par with those produced by commercial publishing companies, in both appearance and content, it hasn't got a chance. Even if it is professional looking, you will still face resistance because the vast majority of bookstores will not work directly with self-publishers. It is too much trouble for them. Just about the only way you can get your book into bookstores is through a book distributor, and finding one to work with you is not an easy task. Distributors are very choosy. And even if a distributor did pick up your book, they will probably put little effort into actively publicizing and promoting it; you still have to do that. Like large publishers, distributors sell all types of books to the same markets (bookstores). They do not give special attention to any of the books, except perhaps a few of the bestsellers.

To be successful in self-publishing you must be very dedicated and spend many hours studying and learning about the business and how to market your books. Before you consider self-publishing, I strongly recommend that you read some of the books available on the subject. Books you should consider reading include: *The Complete Guide to Self-Publishing* by Tom and Marilyn Ross, *The Self-Publishing Manual* by Dan Poynter, and *How to Publish, Promote, and Sell Your Own Book* by Robert Lawrence Holt.

FOREIGN PUBLISHERS

You are not limited to just the publishing companies in this country. You can approach publishers and agents in other countries. Many of them may be more suitable for your book than a domestic press. A spy novel set in Quebec may be of greater interest to a Canadian publisher than one in the United States. A book about Asian sports might be of greater interest to a Japanese press.

The United States produces more books than any other country. American books are found all over the world in both English and non-English speaking countries. Two-thirds of the books sold in Canada, for example, come from the United States. Competition with American publishing companies is so strong that most Canadian publishers focus on books with Canadian content. If you were to seek a Canadian publisher, your chances would be greater if your book's subject was Canadian oriented. The same is true for many other English language publishers, some of which are located in countries where English is not the dominant language.

The greatest markets for most English language manuscripts are English speaking countries, but many other countries where English is commonly spoken also sell and publish English language books.

Your manuscript could be translated into another language by a foreign publisher. If the company has editorial offices or distribution in North America, your book may be produced in both languages. Most foreign publishers do not have American offices. If the publisher doesn't, he may only be interested in obtaining the publishing rights in his native tongue. A publisher in Chile may only be interested in the *Spanish language rights*, which means he has sole right to publish and distribute the book in Spanish language countries.

If a foreign publisher publishes your book, you would have a valuable publishing credit. If he does not want to seek out a publisher to buy the English language rights, you could do it. Resubmit your manuscript to domestic publishers and include information about your foreign publisher.

You can find foreign publishers listed in the *Directory of Book Publishing* (two volumes), *International Literary Market Place*, *International Writer's and Artist's Yearbook*, and *International Directory of Little Magazines and Small Presses*. The first three references also list foreign literary agents. Working with a foreign agent will give you the best chance of finding a suitable publisher.

If you want to contact foreign publishers directly, you should first get a copy of each publisher's author guidelines. The guidelines will explain more fully what each publisher wants and how he wants submissions prepared. In foreign markets, the requirements can vary greatly.

Because of the expense of sending mail out of the country, it would probably be best to send a query letter describing your book before sending a proposal or manuscript. You should also include a self-addressed envelope without stamps. But do include an IRC, obtainable at the post office, which they can redeem for postage in their country.

CHAPTER 12

HOW TO IMPROVE YOUR WRITING

In this book I have made no attempt to teach you the art of writing. The purpose of this book is to teach you how to get what you write published. It has been assumed that your writing is of a quality worthy of publication. In this chapter I will give you some guidance on how to improve your writing and thus increase your chances of getting published. You now know how to get published, the rest depends on the quality and marketability of the material you write.

DEVELOPING LITERARY SKILLS

Manuscripts (as well as query letters and book proposals) are often rejected because they contain spelling, grammar, and punctuation errors, and/or the writing is not particularly interesting or enjoyable to read.

I believe that most new writers think they have a natural writing talent and don't have to go through the processes of studying and practicing to learn their craft. Some people have been able to develop writing skills in the course of their professions or other activities, but most have not. If you possess average writing skills, you can get published by simply following the recommendations outlined in this book. But you are competing with hundreds of other writers at all skill levels. The better your writing is, the greater your chances are of becoming published.

In this book you have learned how to properly prepare your submissions, and how to submit your material. But if you fail to develop your writing skills to a level acceptable to publishers, you will never become published. I have shown you how to avoid the first rounds of rejections and how to get your material into the hands of editors. Your material now must speak for itself and convince the editor that it is worth publishing.

There are many ways you can devlop your writing skills. I will discuss some you should pursue.

Reading and Writing

If you have an interest in writing, you probably have the talent to become a good writer. Two key elements to becoming a good writer are reading good literature and practicing writing.

Read material from people whose style you like. Read a variety of authors and experience the differences in style. Do not try to copy another author's style, but learn what makes writing good and develop your own style.

Practice writing. Write short stories, even if your kids will be the only ones who will hear them; write in a journal or diary, keep a record of interesting observations of life, the people you meet, or your thoughts. Write letters. Do research on subjects of interest. Try your hand at writing articles for community newspapers or newsletters for your church or club.

Write and then rewrite. Rewrite your words as often as necessary, a dozen times if need be, to make your thoughts clear and the words flow smoothly. This is a key element to good writing.

Writer's Support Groups

Join a local writer's support group. These groups meet regularly to talk about different aspects of the writing profession and to critique each other's work. Active membership in such a group can provide invaluable experience to help you develop your writing skills.

These groups usually consist of less than a dozen people. Some may be published authors and some not. The purpose of the group is to help and give encouragement to each other. Members will provide constructive criticism of your writing, and you will do the same for them. You will also keep abreast of any writing workshops, classes, or other opportunities in your area.

Ask your librarian or local high school or college English teachers if there are any writer's groups in your area. Most groups like to limit their size, so even though groups may exist, not all will accept new members.

If there is no literary group available in your area, start your own. Budding writers are everywhere. You will find enough people interested in such a group in most any community. To find them, ask around, or post some flyers announcing your plan in your local library or bookstore.

If your community is too small to form such a group, or you live in isolation, you can form a group which functions by mail. Many writing groups are successful working entirely through the mail. Put a classified advertisement (to keep expenses low) in writer's magazines for interested participants. Or write a letter to the editor of such publications expressing your intentions, and it may be published without cost. Members of a correspondence literary group will exchange writing through the mail. Send your writing to members who will critique it and return it (include a SASE). They will send you their writing in return. Respond with an objective evaluation. You may want to limit the material to 20 or 50 pages so that one person doesn't send that 600-page novel he's been working on for the past 10 years. You should send one or two chapters at a time. Allow a couple of weeks for each evaluation.

Besides local and correspondence literary groups, many national and regional writers' associations can be of great benefit to you. These organizations are dedicated to helping writers perfect their writing skills and learn how to deal with publishers. Many provide newsletters, conferences, workshops, and other helpful aids, as well as networking opportunities. *Literary Market Place* contains a listing of about 70 organizations in the United States and Canada. Some are very general, like the National Writers Club—which is open to all types of writers—while others are geared to more specific interests, like the Mystery Writers of America or Dog Writers' Association. I have listed some of the most popular national organizations in the Appendix. For a more complete listing with a brief annotation on each, see *Literary Market Place*.

Classes

Under the guidance of a competent instructor you can learn a great deal. Most communities offer college or continuing education classes. Take classes in English, literature, writing, and library science. Library science will teach you what materials are available in the library and how to find them.

Even if there are no appropriate classes offered in your area, you may benefit from college level classes. Some colleges and universities offer correspondence courses and give college credit for successfully completing their classes. You may be able to take a class by mail and get feedback on your writing assignments from the English professors.

Many private writing schools and conferences also operate through correspondence courses. You can get instruction and evaluations from well-known authors in many specific areas of writing. For example, if you are interested in writing romance novels, you might work with a successful romance writer; if science fiction is your interest, you could work under an established science fiction writer. If you do not want to be that specific as yet, you may simply choose to work with a teacher of general fiction or nonfiction.

If you have the time and money, you may want to attend a writer's workshop or retreat, going to some out-of-the-way location with a group of other developing writers and spending a week or two with professional writing instructors.

Where do you find these courses and workshops? They are usually advertised in popular writing magazines such as *Writer's Digest* and *The Writer.* You can find these magazines on newsstands or in the library. To find college correspondence courses, ask your local librarian to show you which schools offer such programs.

Magazines and Books

An excellent way to develop writing skills and increase your knowledge of the craft of writing and getting published is to read trade magazines and how-to books on writing.

There are several magazines written for developing writers. The two most popular are *Writer's Digest* and *The Writer*. They contain interesting and thought-provoking articles on all aspects of writing and should be required reading for all authors. Whether you are interested in poetry, fiction, nonfiction, screenplays, or whatever, you will gain valuable insight from these publications.

There are many books on learning how to write and getting published. I highly recommend that you go to your library or bookstore and look at what they have available. Some of the books cover general aspects of writing while others will be very specific. If you want to learn how to write general fiction, there are books which will help you. If you want to focus on developing your mystery writing skills, there are books for that. You can even get more specific and find books for writers on forensic science, weapons, and poisons, which will provide you with background knowledge in these areas so that your writing is accurate and believable.

These books and magazines are very valuable teaching aids and references. I have included an appendix listing the major writer's magazines and some of the many books available that can help you develop your writing skills.

Never stop learning. Keep practicing. Most successful writers will tell you that it took them years to develop their writing skills. They received rejection slips and struggled before they became successful. If you are persistent and strive to develop your writing abilities, you will improve.

LITERARY SERVICES

Book publisher Alfred A. Knopf stated, "We have now reached a point where it becomes more and more difficult to get a reasonable hearing for a book that is simply good—not a world-shattering masterpiece, not the choice of a major book club, not to be made into a super-colossal movie, but just a good book which several thousand Americans would probably read with pleasure and profit from if they ever laid hold of it."

Knopf reveals an interesting aspect of book publishing. Not all good books get published. What gets accepted and what gets rejected is often based on the gut feeling of the editor. In considering two manuscripts for publication when only one can be accepted, the editor must choose the one which has the greatest chance for success. If the manuscripts are equal in this respect, the deciding factor will likely rest with other aspects of the work. This might include the author's ability to express himself clearly and accurately, the quality of the research, available photos, etc.

Many services are available to help writers improve their work and their chances of getting published. With competition as it is, you should take advantage of any opportunity you can to improve your work. Doing so could easily make the difference between receiving a rejection notice or a royalty check.

Typing Service

If you do not have access to a word processor or computer, you should seriously consider using a typing or word processing service. You deliver your writing to them and they will produce a professionally typed product. As I have mentioned in earlier chapters, neatness is important. Having a typing service prepare your material will give it a professional appearance.

If you have a service prepare your manuscript, don't send your only copy to publishers. Make photocopies of it and send the copies. Keep the original.

Research

Publishers look for complete, scholarly research in the writing they publish. Nonfiction works must be accurate and authoritative. Fiction, particularly historical novels, must be based on facts and accurately portray the time period.

If you need information on a particular subject for your book or article, but do not know how to locate it or do not want to spend the time, you can hire the services of a researcher. Researchers are trained to locate information. While it may take you several hours to find the information you need, a researcher may be able to do it in minutes—and will probably be able to give you more detailed information than you could find on your own.

Librarians will be happy to help you if you ask them, but they cannot spend much time with you. They are busy and have other patrons to help. So you cannot monopolize their time. And, in many cases, you will need a good deal of time to track down the information you seek.

Photographs and Illustrations

Having good photos available can make the difference between acceptance and rejection. The key word here is "good" photos. The average person does not normally take publishable pictures. There are many things you must consider when shooting photos; the angle of the sun and shadows, the contrast between the object of the picture and the background, distracting elements in the background, exposure, etc. Most of the photos people send to me are not worth publishing. We can't improve the photos and the reproduction will be of lesser quality than the original. So, if the original photo has poor contrast or is slightly faded or blurred, the reproduction will be worse.

If you cannot produce professional quality photos, have a photographer do it for you. Or buy a book on photography and learn how.

In some cases you will want to use existing photos of famous people, far away places, or historical events. You can obtain such pictures through a stock photo service. Stock photo companies house millions of photos ranging from the present to the first photographs taken a century and a half ago. These photos are compiled from the media as well as from private collections and museums.

Their collections are so extensive that no matter what your subject, they will probably have relevant photos. For instance, if you need a picture of the newest Air Force bomber, or a scene from the latest turmoil in the Middle East or Europe, they will have it. If you need historical pictures, such as Abraham Lincoln delivering the Gettysburg Address or Mark Twain sitting at his desk writing a book, if the picture exists, they probably have it. You simply tell them what you need and they will search their files and send you photocopies of all available prints. They also have drawings. If you need a picture of Alexander Hamilton, who lived before the invention of photography, they can get one for you. This service is not cheap, however, it may cost you as much as $50-$100 per photo.

The United States government also has photo archives, the contents of which are available to anyone for the asking. The Still Picture Section of the National Archives and the Prints & Photographs Division of the Library of Congress have many millions of photos, drawings, and paintings. Since their collections are in the public domain, there is no charge for using them, although you do have to pay a small fee to have prints made. If you are in Washington D.C. you can go to these archives and search for desirable photos yourself, or you can pay a photo researcher to do it for you.

Photo researchers will search government, museum, newspaper, and other private archives for photos. You tell them what kinds of photos you want and they will track them down. Researchers charge by the hour and can usually find suitable photos at a lower cost than photo archive companies. The advantage of the stock photo company is that you know exactly how much you will be charged. With the photo researcher, you won't know until he bills you. This can be even more than the archive service if a great amount of time is needed for your project. You have to pay both the researcher and the institutions or businesses who own the photos. If you give the researcher a limit, he will track down as much material as possible within that budget and then stop. This way you won't end up with a bill larger than you expected.

Critiquing Service

If you send your material to publishers and it is rejected and returned, you will not get an evaluation of the manuscript or any explanation for the rejection other than being told that it "does not meet our current needs." That's all. You will have no idea why they rejected it. If you are lucky, the editor will have liked your material enough to take the time to write you a personal rejection letter and perhaps hint at some areas of improvement.

In most cases you will have no idea why an editor rejects your manuscript. You will keep resubmitting the same manuscript to other publishers who may all reject it for the same reasons. It may not be a bad manuscript. In fact, it may be very good, but have some drawbacks that a little rewriting would correct. You would never know this unless someone with literary knowledge told you.

A literary critic can do this for you. Some literary critics prefer to call themselves manuscript analysts, writing consultants, or book doctors. Whatever name they go by, a literary critic can identify problems, make suggestions for improvement, and offer helpful advice that could make a significant improvement in your work. Although a critic will not point out every misspelled word, incorrect use of punctuation, poor use of grammar, or other mechanical problems, he or she will note that such problems exist. The major function of the critic is to critically evaluate the text in terms of the author's writing style and effectiveness in expressing himself. This evaluation should consist of several pages, although comments could be made directly in the text as well.

A critic looks for many things when evaluating a manuscript. Is the author's writing clear? Would readers understand the descriptions and explanations? (This is particularly important with a how-to or self-help type of book.) Is the vocabulary consistent and appropriate for the readership? (A research scientist writing a book for general audiences would lose readers if he used too much scientific terminology.) Is the material interesting? Does it make the reader want to read more? If it is nonfiction, are the facts and findings presented in an interesting way? Is there supplementary material? (This includes maps, charts, graphs, illustrations, appendix, references, index, footnotes, bibliography, etc.) Are they necessary? Are they adequate or incomplete? Are they effectively and properly presented? Do they make a statement or are they there just to fill space?

For fiction and biography, are the plot and/or subplot(s) clearly defined? Are characters adequately developed? Is suspense or interest maintained throughout the story? Does everything make sense? Is the story believable? Are the facts correct or realistic?

A literary critic can increase a manuscript's chances of publication by pointing out problems. Do not have a friend or relative evaluate your work just to save money. They cannot critique your work objectively. If you enthusiastically hand your friend the novel you've been working on for the past six years, she is not going to be critical. To avoid hurting your feelings and remain a friend, the impromptu critic will compliment your work. Even if your friend did offer you criticism, it would be of questionable worth because, unless she is a professional writer, she won't know how to properly evaluate it.

Literary critics offer a stranger's objective viewpoint. A critic's honest professional feedback may seem disheartening and overly critical. Most writers take pride in their work and tend to seek praise, not criticism. If the evaluation is not complimentary, it is often ignored and the writer feels discouraged or even cheated. She received what she paid for, but did not receive what she wanted. If you use a critique service, you must have an open mind and be able to accept criticism. If you have questions about the critique, most critics will be willing to discuss them with you. If you seriously doubt some of the critic's recommendations or comments, ask someone who is familiar with your work to either confirm or dispute them. Whether or not you follow the critic's advice is up to you. Although they are professionals, you must make the final decision yourself.

Editing and Proofreading Services

I have saved for last probably the most important service you can use—copyediting and proofreading services. The primary reason most manuscripts are rejected is they do not meet the standards of publication. Publishers receive so many manuscripts that they can be very choosy. Some are extremely picky and will not even consider material that is not close to being perfect.

Having a knowledgeable editor read and correct your work is the most valuable service you can receive. While a literary critic will make suggestions on revisions concerning content and style, an editor will actually make detailed corrections in your text.

Proofreaders look for and correct spelling, punctuation, grammatical, typographical, and other mechanical errors. A copyeditor's job includes everything a proofreader does, but goes one step further. In addition to making mechanical corrections, the copyeditor corrects literary errors. These include correcting inconsistencies in style and awkward sentence structure, and clarifying sentences, words, or ideas not clearly expressed by the writer. The copyeditor works on sentence structure, phrases, and word choice to make the text flow smoother.

Usually proofreaders read material which is nearly finished and laid out in its final format. Copyeditors, on the other hand, are the ones who make the initial corrections and preparations on manuscripts. The biggest difference resulting from making corrections at different stages of the development of the text is that initially, the material will have more errors and require more corrections by the copyeditor than it will by the proofreader.

I strongly recommend that every writer, no matter what his or her skill level is, have their work reviewed by an experienced editor before sending it to publishers. When I say experienced editor, I don't mean friends or relatives. These people are often not sufficiently qualified to do this type of work. They may catch obvious errors, but there is much more to proofreading and editing than spotting simple typographical errors. Some people depend too much on computer software programs designed to check for spelling and grammatical errors for their editing needs. But such programs should not be a substitute for having material proofread. The computer programs will catch simple errors, but pass over words spelled correctly but used incorrectly in the text. It takes a human to catch these types of errors.

Editing provides a second educated opinion or viewpoint. Many statements that make sense to you may not be clear to someone who is unfamiliar with the subject. An editor can point out these problems. Writers become so familiar with their own material that they tend to see only what they want to see. I know this through experience. I have read my own short copy over and over, looking for errors, and then handed it to someone else who quickly points out obvious typos. All writers experience this.

As a publisher, I have never received a manuscript that did not need editing. Some have needed only a little, but most need a lot. Even English teachers, newspaper reporters, and others who work in the literary world can benefit from a professional editing job.

I cannot stress enough the importance of using an editor to improve your work. If you are already a successful author who has no trouble getting published without using an independent editor, then you probably don't need one. I remember reading about one famous author with dozens of bestsellers to his credit who routinely has five independent editors read and evaluate his work before he sends it to his publisher. This person knows the value of editorial services. He is also published and very successful.

Proofreader's Marks

When working with copyeditors and proofreaders you should, if possible, give them your manuscript in the same format you would send to a publisher—neatly typed and double-spaced with ample room around the margins. The extra space is necessary for them to make corrections and write comments.

Proofreader's marks are shorthand notations for specific corrections. If every correction had to be written out, it would be very time consuming and messy. Editors and proofreaders use the same marks. Copyeditors commonly make corrections within the text while proofreaders indicate where errors are in the text, but make the corrections in the margin. The primary reason for this is that editors work with copy that is double-spaced, so there is room between the lines to make corrections. Proofreaders often work with material that is single-spaced.

Most of the proofreader's marks are standard and easily recognized by editors, publishers, and writers. If you work with freelance copyeditors and proofreaders, you will need to become familiar with proofreader's marks. You must also know them in order to communicate effectively with your publisher. Book and magazine editors may copyedit your manuscript and send it back to you for revision. Also, if the publisher sends you a galley proof to review before the book or article is published, you should be able to mark corrections on the proof using standard proofreader's marks so that they understand exactly what changes you want. Standard proofreading marks you will see most often are listed in Table 1.

A caret (^) in the text is used to flag an insertion of a word, letter, and most punctuation marks. Draw the caret at the bottom of the line where the insertion is to be made. An inverted caret (∨) is placed inside the text to indicate the insertion of an apostrophe, quotation mark, superscript, or asterisk.

Circling is used in the margins with proofreader's marks

TABLE 1

Mark in Margin	Mark in Text	Explanation	Corrected Text
ℯ	the freelance writerr	remove letter	the freelance writer
⁀	the fre elance writer	close up	the freelance writer
(stet)	the ~~freelance~~ writer	let it stay	the freelance writer
(lc)	The freelance writer	lowercase letter	the freelance writer
(lc)/(3)	The Freelance Writer	lowercase letter	the freelance writer
(lc)	THE freelance writer	lowercase word	the freelance writer
(rule)	the freelance writer	underline	the <u>freelance</u> writer
(ital)	the freelance writer	italicize	the *freelance* writer
(bf)	the freelance writer	boldface type	the **freelance** writer
(cap)	the freelance writer	capitalize letter	The freelance writer
(tr)	hte freelance writer	transpose	the freelance writer
¶	She is the freelance writer. Careful reading is necessary.	new paragraph	She is the freelance writer. Careful reading is necessary.
No ¶	She is the freelance writer. Careful reading is necessary.	same paragraph	She is the freelance writer. Careful reading is necessary.
#	the freelancewriter	insert space	the freelance writer
(?)	the freelance writers	query to author	the freelance writer

Mark in Margin	Mark in Text	Explanation	Corrected Text
?	the freelance writer ^	insert question mark	the freelance writer?
⊙	the freelance writer ^	insert period	the freelance writer.
(:)	the freelance writer ^	insert colon	the freelance writer:
^ ,	the younger ^ freelance writer	insert comma	the younger, freelance writer
^ ;	the freelance writer ^ the younger writer	add semicolon	the freelance writer; the younger writer
'	the writers work	add apostrophe	the writer's work
" / "	the freelance writer	insert quotation marks	"the freelance writer"
(/)	the ^ freelance ^ writer	add parentheses	the (freelance) writer
1/m	proofreading-as noted above	long dash (not hyphen)	proofreading—as noted above
=	the free ^ lance writer	add hyphen	the free-lance writer
‖	the freelance writer	even out lines	the freelance writer
[	[the freelance writer	move left	the freelance writer
]	the freelance writer]	move right	the freelance writer
(SP)	(3) freelance writers	spell out word	three freelance writers

for clarification. Some confusion might occur between words of instruction to the typesetter and words that are to be added to the text. To avoid ambiguity, instructions to the typesetter are always circled. Words or letters that are to be added to the text are not. An exception to this rule is with periods and colons. Periods and colons are circled because they are so small they might otherwise be overlooked.

Circles are also used inside the text around a word or letter to be corrected. Never circle words that are to be typed or typeset in the final copy.

HOW TO FIND HELP

In this chapter I have discussed many different types of services available to you that will improve or enhance your work. You can find the individuals and companies who offer many of these services in the directory *Literary Market Place*. This reference book lists publishers, agents, ghost writers, interviewing services, manuscript analysts, researchers, writing groups, and many others involved in the book industry. This directory is expensive so you're not likely to find it in a bookstore. Most good sized libraries will have a copy in their reference section. Another directory which lists writing services is the *Book Publishing Resource Guide* (Ad-Lib Publications).

The Editorial Freelancers Association (Box 2050, Madison Square Station, New York, NY 10159) and the Freelance Editorial Association (P.O. Box 835, Cambridge, MA 02238) can provide you a list of people offering editoral services to writers and publishers.

Another source for these services is writer's magazines. Look in the back of the magazines near the classified ad section. Often the ad listings will be categorized so that if you want to find research services, look under "Research," or find copyediting services under "Editing/Revising" and so forth. These magazines also contain ads for subsidy publishing, literary agents, self-publishing services, as well as writer's workshops and correspondence schools and seminars. These magazines provide an abundance of information that would be of benefit to you as a writer. I recommend that you subscribe to one or more of them. Read them, use the services offered in them, read good literature, and write! I have included the names and addresses of several writers magazines as well as directories listing useful services for writers in the Appendix.

As you are writing, you may have questions on grammar, punctuation, or word choice and usage. You can get these questions answered quickly through a grammar hotline. There are about 60 hotlines throughout the country run on a volunteer basis. Most hotlines are operated free of charge by colleges or teachers as a public service to writers and students. Each hotline has its own hours. Some are closed during the summer. To get a copy of the *Grammar Hotline Directory* send a self-addressed envelope with one first class stamp to Grammar Hotline, Tidewater Community College, 1700 College Crescent, Virginia Beach, VA 23456.

Becoming A Successful Author

There have been several notable works from first-time authors in recent years. Amy Tan's bestselling *The Joy Luck Club* brought a $50,000 advance and was made into a major motion picture. Other novels from first-time authors which became blockbuster bestsellers include: Naomi Ragen's *Jephte's Daughters*, Bryce Courtenay's *The Power of One*, John Lucas's *Tables*, Judith Merkle Riley's *A Vision of Light*, Tom Clancy's *The Hunt for Red October*, Scott Turow's *Presumed Innocent*, and Michael Chabon's *Mysteries of Pittsburgh*.

Fueled by the success of these first-time novelists, unpublished writers dream of huge advances and bestseller status. Most successful novelists, however, become so very gradually. Their early works often remain unpublished. They build an audience as more books are published, receiving big money only after the fourth or fifth book. Most advances for works by first-time authors are less than $5,000 and if published by a large or medium-sized house, will probably go out of print after a single printing. Most successful authors work very hard yet never get rich.

Chet Cunningham is a typical example of a successful writer. He sold his first novel, a western, in 1968 for a grand total of $300. It wasn't a bestseller. None of his works have been considered blockbusters. He has never signed a two book contract for $12.4 million. But he has sold 225 books, over 1,300 magazine articles, and for the past 30 years has earned a living as a writer.

"I didn't publish a bestselling novel the year I got out of college," Cunningham says. "I wasn't one of those instant successes." He took "bonehead" English when he started college. He wanted to major in journalism, but the journalism professor didn't want him. Cunningham explains that they were short of majors that year so he got his wish. After graduating he turned to newspapers because they offered a regular paycheck. He worked as a reporter for two years and in his spare time tried to write the great American War Novel about his Korean experiences. It was never published.

He found a new job as an audiovisual writer and wrote short stories and magazine articles during evenings and weekends. "I never was hailed as a promising young writer," he said. "But I eventually learned how to freelance trade journal articles." His first article sold for $20. His first year of freelancing earned him the proud sum of $102. For six years he worked all day at his job, came home and worked half the night on freelance writing. When he was laid off from his job he tried freelancing full time. He sold his first novel eight years later.

"Most of us work long and hard to learn the craft," Cunningham says. There is no easy road to success. "I learned to specialize. I've sold 100 western novels." Very few bookstores don't have at least one of his westerns.

"Specialize, build a name in a field," Cunningham advises. "Get editors to know you and your work in that field. The best suggestion of all is try to write series books. Don't write one book about a character, do a dozen... Series make for a long writing life, and a steady income."

It's easy for new writers to get discouraged. Success doesn't come easily. Cunningham says, "You say you've written *two* complete novels and haven't sold even one. Hey, poor you. Most novelists write five or six before they sell one. The secret is to write to a *market*. Don't just write what you want to write, especially if you're trying to sell... Plan on writing to sell, not just writing. There's a difference. Writing to sell is done with a plan, a market, knowing the requirements, the length, the viewpoint. You can write to sell only when you know your genre inside out and upside down."

To be successful, Cunningham strongly advises new writers to put a great deal of time and effort into learning the craft. "Work your tail off. Don't expect the writing life to be an easy three hours a day, followed by parties, publishers' teas, and book signings. Rather, you'll need to be willing to put in ten to twelve hours a day at your machine, to write until your teeth fall out and your eyes cross in back of your head. If you work a full day at another job, plan to spend at least an additional four hours a day writing.

"Is there another way? Sure, be a genius, a publishing phenomenon. There just aren't many around these days though. I wasn't one, but I succeeded. And if I did it, you can do it."

APPENDIX

RESOURCES

DIRECTORIES

Listed below are the major trade directories useful to writers. Few of them can be found in your local bookstore. Many will be in any good sized library. If you can't find one in your area you can write to the publisher to obtain a copy.

North American Directories

The Association of American University Presses Directory, University of Chicago Press, 5801 Ellis Ave., 4th Fl., Chicago IL 60637

The Book Trade in Canada/L'Industrie du Livre au Canada, Ampersand Communications Services, Inc., 2766 Sheffield Rd., Ottawa ON, K1B 3V9 Canada

California Publishing Marketplace, Writers Connection, 1601 Saratoga-Sunnyvale Rd. #180, Cupertino, CA 95014

Canadian Publishers Directory, Quill & Quire Magazine, 70 The Esplanade, 4th Fl., Toronto ON, M5E 1RA Canada

Canadian Writer's Guide, Fitzhenry & Whiteside, 195 Allstate Parkway, Markham, ON, L3R 4T8 Canada

Canadian Writer's Market, McClelland & Stewart, 481 University Ave., Suite 900, Toronto, ON, M5G 2E9 Canada

Children's Media Market Place, Neal-Schuman Publishers, 100 Varick St., New York, NY 10013

Children's Writer's & Illustrator's Market, Writer's Digest Books, 1507 Dana Avenue, Cincinnati, OH 45207

Christian Writer's Market Guide, Joy Publishing, P.O. Box 827, San Juan Capistrano, CA 92675

Directory of Book Publishing, Oryx Press, 4041 N. Central, Phoenix, AZ 85012

Directory of Florida Markets for Writers and PR Professionals, Cassell Communications, P.O. Box 9844, Fort Lauderdale, FL 33310

Directory of Poetry Publishers, Dustbooks, P.O. Box 100, Paradise, CA 95969

Directory of Publications Resources, Editorial Experts, Inc., 66 Canal Center Plaza, Suite 200, Alexandria, VA 22314

Dramatist's Sourcebook, Theatre Communications Group, 355 Lexington Ave., New York, NY 10017

Encyclopedia of Associations, Gale Research, 835 Penobscot Bldg., Detroit, MI 48226-4094

Freelance Editorial Association Yellow Pages, Freelance Editorial Association, P.O. Box 835, Cambridge, MA 02238

Guide to Literary Agents and Art/Photo Reps, Writer's Digest Books, 1507 Dana Avenue, Cincinnati, OH 45207

Humor & Cartoon Markets, Writer's Digest Books, 1507 Dana Avenue, Cincinnati, OH 45207

Literary Agents of North America: The Complete Guide to U.S. and Canadian Literary Agencies, Author Aid Associates, 340 E. 52nd St., New York, NY 10022

Literary Market Place, R.R. Bowker, 121 Chanlon Road, New Providence, NJ 07974

Market Guide for Young Writers, Writer's Digest Books, 1507 Dana Avenue, Cincinnati, OH 45207

Mystery Writer's Market Place and Sourcebook, 1507 Dana Avenue, Cincinnati, OH 45207

Novel and Short Story Writer's Market, Writer's Digest Books, 1507 Dana Avenue, Cincinnati, OH 45207

Northwest Publishing Market Place, Writer's Connection, 1601 Saratoga-Sunnyvale Road #180, Cupertino, CA 95014

Poet's Handbook, Fine Arts Press, P.O. Box 3491, Knoxville, TN 37927

Poet's Market, Writer's Digest Books, 1507 Dana Avenue, Cincinnati, OH 45207

The Poet's Marketplace, Running Press, 125 S. 22nd St., Philadelphia, PA 19103

Religious Writer's Marketplace, Running Press, 125 S. 22nd St., Philadelphia, PA 19103

Scriptwriters Market, Script Writers-Filmmakers Publishing, 8033 Sunset Blvd., Suite 306, Hollywood, CA 90046

Southwest Publishing Market Place, Writer's Connection, 1601 Saratoga-Sunnyvale Road #180, Cupertino, CA 95014

Travel Writer's Markets, Harvard Common Press, 535 Albany Street, Boston, MA 02118

Writing for the Ethnic Markets, Writer's Connection, 1601 Saratoga-Sunnyvale Rd #180, Cupertino, CA 95014

The Writer's Handbook, The Writer, 120 Boylston Street, Boston, MA 02116

Writer's Market, Writer's Digest Books, 1507 Dana Avenue, Cincinnati, OH 45207

Writer's Northwest Handbook, Media Weavers, 24450 NW Hansen Road, Hillsboro, OR 97124

The Writer's Yellow Pages, Steve Davis Publishing, P.O. Box 190831, Dallas, TX 75219

British, Australian, and International Directories

Australian and New Zealand Booksellers and Publishers, D.W. Thorpe, 18 Salmon Street, Port Melbourne, Victoria 3207 Australia

Directory of Book Publishers and Wholesalers, Booksellers Association of Great Britain and Ireland, 272 Vauxhall Bridge Road, London SW1V 1BA, UK

International Directory of Little Magazines and Small Presses, Dustbooks, P.O. Box 100, Paradise, CA 95969, USA

International Literary Market Place, R.R. Bowker, 121 Chanlon Road, New Providence, NJ 07974, USA

International Writers' & Artists' Yearbook, A&C Black Ltd., 35 Bedford Row, London, WC1 4JH England (distributed in the U.S. by Writer's Digest Books)

Publishers in the United Kingdom and their Addresses, J. Whitaker and Sons Ltd., 12 Dyott Street, London WC1A 1DF, UK

Writers and Photographers Marketing Guide: Directory of Australian and New Zealand Literary and Photo Markets, Australian Writers and Professional Service, Stott House, 140 Flinders Street, Melbourne, Victoria 3000 Australia

NATIONAL WRITER'S ORGANIZATIONS

This is a partial list of the major national and international writers organizations in North America. For a more complete listing, including many regional organizations, see *Literary Market Place*. For a detailed listing of organizations outside North America see *International Literary Market Place*.

Authors Guild, 330 W. 42nd Street, New York, NY 10036

Canadian Authors Association, 104 - 121 Avenue Rd., Toronto, ON M5R 2G3 Canada

Christian Writers Guild, 260 Fern Lane, Hume, CA 93628

Council of Writers Organizations, 1 Auto Club Dr., Dearborn, MI 48126

International Association of Crime Writers, Inc. (North America Branch), JAF Box 1500, New York, NY 10116

International Society of Dramatists, P.O. Box 1310, Miami, FL 33153

The International Womans Writing Guild, Box 810, Gracie Sta., New York, NY 10028

Mystery Writers of America, 17 E. 47th Street, 6th Fl, New York, NY 10017

National League of American Pen Women, Inc., 1300 17th St. NW, Washington, DC 20036-1973

The National Writers Club, Inc., 1450 S. Havana, Suite 620, Aurora, CO 80012

National Writers Union, 873 Broadway, Suite 203, New York, NY 10003

Outdoor Writers' Association of America, 2017 Cato Ave., Suite 101, State College, PA 16801

PEN American Center, 568 Broadway, New York, NY 10012

Periodical Writers' Association of Canada, Writers' Centre, 24 Ryerson Ave., Toronto, ON, M5T 2P3 Canada

Romance Writers of America, 13700 Veterans Memorial Dr., Suite 315, Houston TX 77014

Science Fiction-Fantasy Writers of America, Inc., 5 Winding Brook Dr., Suite 1B, Guilderland, NY 12084

Society of American Travel Writers, 1155 Connecticut Ave NW, Suite 500, Washington, DC 20036

WRITER'S MAGAZINES

This is a list of the major writer's magazines in North America. Write to them for additional information about content and subscritions.

Byline, P.O. Box 130596, Edmond, OK 73013

Canadian Author & Bookman, 121 Avenue Rd., Suite 104, Toronto, ON, M5R 2G3 Canada

The Comedy Writers Association Newsletter, Box 023304, Brooklyn, NY 11202

Freelance Writer's Report, P.O. Box 9844, Fort Lauderdale, FL 33310

Housewife-Writer's Forum, P.O. Box 780, Lyman, WY 82937

New Writer's Magazine, P.O. Box 5976, Sarasota, FL 34277

Scavenger's Newsletter, 519 Ellinwood, Osage City, KS 66523

Science Fiction Chronicle, P.O. Box 2730, Brooklyn, NY 11202

The Writer, 120 Boylston St., Boston, MA 02116

Writers Connection, P.O. Box 24770, San Jose, CA 95154

Writer's Digest, 1507 Dana Ave., Cincinnati, OH 45207

Writer's Guidelines, P.O. Box 608, Pittsburg, MO 65724

Writer's Journal, 27 Empire Dr., St. Paul, MN 55103

Writer's Lifeline, Box 32, Cornwall, ON, K6H 5R9 Canada

The Writer's Nook News, 38114 3rd St. #181, Willoughby, OH 44094

Writer's NW, 24450 NW Hansen Rd., Hillsboro, OR 97124

CONFERENCES AND WORKSHOPS

Listed here are some resources for locating writers' conferences, workshops, and correspondence courses.

Author & Audience: A Readings and Workshops Guide, Poets & Writers, Inc., 72 Spring St., New York, NY10012

The AWP Official Guide to Writing Programs, Dustbooks, P.O. Box 100, Paradise, CA 95967

The Correspondence Educational Directory, Racz Publishing, 6000 S. Eastern Ave., Bldg. 7, Suite D, Las Vegas, NV 89119

The Guide to Writers Conferences, Shaw Associates, Publishers, 625 Biltmore Way #1406, Coral Gables, FL 33134

Writers Conferences, Poets & Writers, Inc., 72 Spring St., New York, NY 10012

The Writer's Essential Desk Reference, Writer's Digest Books, 1507 Dana Ave., Cincinnati, OH 45207

INDEX